Pre.

LOVE'S
LABOUR'S LOST

Foreword by
Richard Eyre

NT
NATIONAL

NICK HERN BOOKS

First published in this collected paperback edition in 1993 jointly by
Nick Hern Books Limited, 14 Larden Road, London W3 7ST
and the Royal National Theatre, London,
by arrangement with Batsford.

Preface to Love's Labour's Lost. Originally published in 1924, revised
1927

Set in 10/11 Baskerville by Pure Tech Corporation, Pondicherry
(India)
Printed in Australia by
Australian Print Group

A CIP catalogue record for this book is available from the British
Library

ISBN 1 85459 112 6

Shakespeare Alive!

The history of the theatre in England in this century can be told largely through the lives and work of two men: George Bernard Shaw and Harley Granville Barker, a triple-barrelled cadence of names that resonates like the ruffling of the pages of a large book in a silent public library. One was a brilliant polemicist who dealt with certainties and assertions and sometimes, but not often enough, breathed life into his sermons; the other a committed sceptic who started from the premise that the only thing certain about human behaviour was that nothing was certain. Both, however, possessed a passionate certainty about the importance of the theatre and the need to revise its form, its content, and the way that it was managed. Shaw was a playwright, critic and pamphleteer, Barker a playwright, director and actor.

The Voysey Inheritance is, at least in my opinion, Granville Barker's best play: a complex web of family relationships, a fervent but never unambiguous indictment of a world dominated by the mutually dependent obsessions of greed, class, and self-deception. It's also a virtuoso display of stagecraft: the writer showing that as director he can handle twelve speaking characters on stage at one time, and that as actor he can deal with the most ambitious and unexpected modulations of thought and feeling. The 'inheritance' of the Voyseys is a legacy of debt, bad faith, and bitter family dissension. Edward's father has, shortly before his death, revealed that he has been cheating the family firm of solicitors for many years, as his father had for many years before that. Towards the end of the play Edward Voysey, the youngest son, confronts the woman he loves:

> EDWARD.   Why wouldn't he own the truth to me about himself?
>
> BEATRICE.   Perhaps he took care not to know it. Would you have understood?
>
> EDWARD.   Perhaps not. But I loved him.
>
> BEATRICE.   That would silence a bench of judges.

Shaw would have used the story to moralise and polemicise. He might have had the son hate the father; he might have had him forgive him; he might have had him indict him as a paradigm of capitalism; he would never have said he loved him.

Everybody needs a father, or, failing that, a father-figure. He may be a teacher, a prophet, a boss, a priest perhaps, a political leader, a friend, or, sometimes, if you are very lucky, the real one. If you can't find a father you must invent him. In some ways, not altogether trivial, Granville Barker is something of a father-figure for me. He's a writer whom I admire more than any twentieth-century English writer before the sixties – Chekhov with an English accent; he's the first modern British director; he's the real founder of the National Theatre and, in his *Prefaces*, he's a man who, alone amongst Shakespearean commentators before Jan Kott, believed in the power of Shakespeare on stage.

There was a myth that Granville Barker was the natural son of Shaw. He was certainly someone whom Shaw could, in his awkward way, cherish and admire, educate and castigate. When Barker fell wildly in love ('in the Italian manner' as Shaw said) with Helen Huntington, an American millionairess, he married her, acquired a hyphen in his surname, moved first to Devon to play the part of a country squire, and then to France to a life of seclusion. Shaw thought that he had buried himself alive and could never reconcile himself to the loss. It was, as his biographer

Hesketh Pearson said: 'The only important matter about which he asked me to be reticent.'

After directing many of Shaw's plays for many years, acting many of his best roles (written by Shaw with Barker in mind), dreaming and planning together the birth of a National Theatre, not to mention writing, directing, and acting in his own plays while managing his own company at the Royal Court, Barker withdrew from the theatre, and for twenty years there was silence between the two men. Only on the occasion of the death of Shaw's wife did they communicate by letters. 'I did not know I could be so moved by anything,' wrote Shaw to him.

Out of this self-exile came one major work, slowly assembled over many years: *The Prefaces to Shakespeare*. With a few exceptions (Auden on *Othello*, Barbara Everett on *Hamlet*, Jan Kott on *The Tempest*) it's the only critical work about Shakespeare that's made any impact on me, apart, that is, from my father's view of Shakespeare, which was brief and brutal: 'It's absolute balls.'

As much as we need a good father, we need a good teacher. Mine, improbably perhaps, was Kingsley Amis. He'd arrived, somewhat diffidently, at Cambridge at the same time as I did. The depth of my ignorance of English literature corresponded almost exactly to his dislike of the theatre. Nevertheless, he made me see Shakespeare with a mind uncontaminated by the views of academics, whom he would never have described as his fellows and whose views he regarded as, well, academic. I would write essays marinated in the opinions of Spurgeon, Wilson Knight, Dover Wilson and a large cast of critical supernumeraries. He would gently, but courteously, cast aside my essay about, say, *Twelfth Night*: 'But what do *you* think of this play? Do you think it's any good?' 'Well ... er ... it's Shakespeare.' 'Yes, but is it any *good*? I mean as a *play*. It says it's a comedy. Fine. But does it have any decent jokes?'

I took this for irreverence, heresy even. Over the years, however, I've come to regard this as good teaching, or, closely allied, good direction. It's asking the right questions, unintimidated by reputation, by tradition, by received opinion, or by critical orthodoxy. This was shocking, but healthy, for a young and impressionable man ripe to become a fundamentalist in matters of literary taste and ready to revere F. R. Leavis as the Ayatollah of 'Cambridge English'. What you have is yourself and the text, only that. That's the lesson of Granville Barker: 'We have the text to guide us, half a dozen stage directions, and that is all. I abide by the text and the demands of the text and beyond that I claim freedom.' I can't imagine a more useful and more enduring dictum.

The Prefaces have a practical aim: 'I want to see Shakespeare made fully effective on the English stage. That is the best sort of help I can lend.' What Granville Barker wrote is a primer for directors and actors working on the plays of Shakespeare. There is lamentably little useful literature about the making of theatre, even though there is an indigestible glut of memoirs and biographies, largely concerned with events that have taken place *after* the curtain has fallen. If I was asked by a visiting Martian to recommend books which would help him, her or it to make theatre in the manner of the European I could only offer four books: Stanislavsky on *The Art of the Stage*, John Willett's *Brecht on Theatre*, Peter Brook's *The Empty Space*, and *The Prefaces to Shakespeare*.

Stanislavsky offers a pseudo-scientific dissection of the art of acting which is, in some respects, like reading Freud on the mechanism of the joke: earnest, well-meaning, but devoid of the indispensable ingredient of its subject matter: humour. Stanislavsky's great contribution was to demand that actors hold the mirror up to nature, that they take their craft as seriously as the writers they served, and to provide some sort of formal discipline within which both aims could be realised.

Brecht provided a manifesto that was a political and aesthetic response to the baroque encrustations of the scenery-laden, star-dominated, archaic boulevard theatre of Germany in the twenties. Although much of what he wrote as theory is an unpalatable mix of political ideology and artistic instruction, it is his theatrical instinct that prevails. He asserts, he insists, he browbeats. He demands that the stage, like society, must be re-examined, reformed, that the audience's habits mustn't be satisfied, they must be changed, but just when he is about to nail his 13 Articles to the church door he drops the voice of the zealot: 'The stage is not a hothouse or a zoological museum full of stuffed animals. It must be peopled with live, three-dimensional self-contradictory people with their passions, unconsidered utterances and actions.' In all art forms, he says, the guardians of orthodoxy will assert that there are eternal and immutable laws that you ignore at your peril, but in the theatre there is only one inflexible rule: 'The proof of the pudding is in the eating.' Brecht teaches us to ask the question: what goes on in a theatre?

Brook takes that question even further: what *is* theatre? It's a philosophical, but eminently practical, question that Brook has been asking for over 30 years and which has taken him to the African desert, a quarry in Iran, and an abandoned music hall in Paris. 'I take an empty space and call it a bare stage. A man walks across this empty space while someone else is watching him, and that is all that is needed for an act of theatre to be engaged.' For all his apparent concern with metaphyics, there is no more practical man of the theatre than Brook.

I was once at a seminar where someone asked him what was the job of the director. 'To get the actors on and off stage,' he said. Like Brecht, like Stanislavsky, like Granville Barker, Brook argues that for the theatre to be expressive it must be, above all, simple and unaffected: a distillation of language, of gesture, of action, of design, where meaning is the essence. The meaning must be felt as much as understood. 'They don't have to understand with their ears,' says Granville Barker, 'just with their guts.'

Brecht did not acknowledge a debt to Granville Barker. Perhaps he was not aware of one, but it seems to me that Barker's Shakespeare productions were the direct antecedents of Brecht's work. He certainly knew enough about English theatre to know that he was on to a good thing adapting *The Beggar's Opera, The Recruiting Officer* and *Coriolanus*. Brecht has been lauded for destroying illusionism; Granville Barker has been unhymned. He aimed at re-establishing the relationship between actor and audience that had existed in Shakespeare's theatre – and this at a time when the prevailing style of Shakespearean production involved *not* stopping short of having live sheep in *As You Like It*. He abolished footlights and the proscenium arch, building out an apron over the orchestra pit which Shaw said 'apparently trebled the spaciousness of the stage. . . . To the imagination it looks as if he had invented a new heaven and a new earth.'

His response to staging Shakespeare was not to look for a synthetic Elizabethanism. 'We shall not save our souls by being Elizabethan.' To recreate the Globe would, he knew, be aesthetic anasthaesia, involving the audience in an insincere conspiracy to pretend that they were willing collaborators in a vain effort to turn the clock back. His answers to staging Shakespeare were similar to Brecht's for *his* plays and, in some senses, to

Chekhov's for his. He wanted scenery not to decorate and be literal, but to be expressive and metaphorical, and at the same time, in apparent contradiction, to be specific and be real, while being minimal and iconographic: the cart in *Mother Courage*, the nursery in *The Cherry Orchard*, the dining table in *The Voysey Inheritance*. 'To create a new hieroglyphic language of scenery. That, in a phrase, is the problem. If the designer finds himself competing with the actors, the sole interpreters Shakespeare has licensed, then it is he that is the intruder and must retire.'

In *The Prefaces* Granville Barker argues for a fluency of staging unbroken by scene changes. Likewise the verse should be spoken fast. 'Be swift, be swift, be not poetical,' he wrote on the dressing-room mirror of Cathleen Nesbitt when she played Perdita. Within the speed, however, detailed reality. *Meaning* above all.

It is the director's task, with the actors, to illuminate the meanings of a play: its vocabulary, its syntax, and its philosophy. The director has to ask what each scene is revealing about the characters and their actions: what story is each scene telling us? In *The Prefaces* Granville Barker exhumes, examines and explains the lost stagecraft of Shakespeare line by line, scene by scene, play by play.

Directing Shakespeare is a matter of understanding the meaning of a scene and staging it in the light of that knowledge. Easier said than done, but it's at the heart of the business of directing any play, and directing Shakespeare is merely directing writ large. Beyond that, as David Mamet has observed, 'choice of actions and adverbs constitute the craft of directing'. Get up from that chair and walk across the room. Slowly.

With Shakespeare as with any other playwright the director's job is to make the play live, now, in the present tense. 'Spontaneous enjoyment is the life of the theatre,' says Granville Barker in his Preface to *Love's Labour's Lost*. To receive a review, as Granville Barker did, headed *SHAKESPEARE ALIVE!* is the most, but should be the least, that a director must hope for.

I regard Granville Barker not only as the first modern English director but as the most influential. Curiously, partly as a result of his early withdrawal from the theatre, partly because his *Prefaces* have been out of print for many years, and partly because of his own self-effacement, he has been unjustly ignored both in the theatre and in the academic world, where the codification of their 'systems' has resulted in the canonisation of Brecht and Stanislavsky. I hope the re-publication of *The Prefaces* will right the balance. Granville Barker himself always thought of them as his permanent legacy to the theatre.

My sense of filial identification is not entirely a professional one. When I directed *The Voysey Inheritance* I wanted a photograph of the author on the poster. A number of people protested that it was the height, or depth, of vanity and self-aggrandisement to put my own photograph on the poster. I was astonished, I was bewildered, but I was not unflattered. I still can't see the resemblance, but it's not through lack of trying.

Two years ago the Royal National Theatre was presented with a wonderful bronze bust of Granville Barker by Katherine Scott (the wife, incidentally, of the Antarctic hero). For a while it sat on the windowsill of my office like a benign houschold god. Then it was installed on a bracket in the foyer opposite a bust of Olivier, the two men eyeing each other in wary mutual regard. A few months later it was stolen; an act of homage perhaps. I miss him.

Richard Eyre

Introduction

We have still much to learn about Shakespeare the playwright. Strange that it should be so, after three centuries of commentary and performance, but explicable. For the Procrustean methods of a changed theatre deformed the plays, and put the art of them to confusion; and scholars, with this much excuse, have been apt to divorce their Shakespeare from the theatre altogether, to think him a poet whose use of the stage was quite incidental, whose glory had small relation to it, for whose lapses it was to blame.

The Study and the Stage

THIS much is to be said for Garrick and his predecessors and successors in the practice of reshaping Shakespeare's work to the theatre of their time. The essence of it was living drama to them, and they meant to keep it alive for their public. They wanted to avoid whatever would provoke question and so check that spontaneity of response upon which acted drama depends. Garrick saw the plays, with their lack of 'art', through the spectacles of contemporary culture; and the bare Elizabethan stage, if it met his mind's eye at all, doubtless as a barbarous makeshift. Shakespeare was for him a problem; he tackled it, from our point of view, misguidedly and with an overplus of enthusiasm. His was a positive world; too near in time, moreover, as well as too opposed in taste to Shakespeare's to treat it perspectively. The romantic movement might have brought a more concordant outlook. But by then the scholars were off their own way; while the theatre began to think of its Shakespeare from the point of view of the picturesque, and, later, in terms of upholstery. Nineteenth-century drama developed along the lines of realistic illusion, and the staging of Shakespeare was further subdued to this, with inevitably disastrous effect on the speaking of his verse; there was less perversion of text perhaps, but actually more wrenching of the construction of the plays for the convenience of the stage carpenter. The public appetite for this sort of thing having been gorged, producers then turned to newer—and older—contrivances, leaving 'realism' (so called) to the modern comedy that had fathered it. Amid much vaporous theorizing—but let us humbly own how hard it is not to write nonsense about art, which seems ever pleading to be enjoyed and not written about at all—the surprising discovery had been made that varieties of stagecraft and stage were not historical accidents but artistic obligations, that Greek drama belonged in a Greek theatre, that Elizabethan plays, therefore, would, presumably, do best upon an Elizabethan stage, that there was nothing sacrosanct about scenery, footlights, drop-curtain or any of their belongings. This brings us to the present situation.

There are few enough Greek theatres in which Greek tragedy can be played; few enough people want to see it, and they will applaud it encouragingly however it is done. Some acknowledgement is due to the altruism of the doers! Shakespeare is another matter. The English theatre, doubtful of its destiny, of necessity venal, opening its doors to all comers, seems yet, as by some instinct, to seek renewal of strength in him. An actor, unless success has made him cynical, or his talent be merely trivial, may take some pride in the hall mark of Shakespearean achievement. So may a manager if he thinks he can afford it. The public (or their spokesmen) seem to consider Shakespeare and his genius a sort of national property, which, truly, they do nothing to conserve, but in which they have moral rights not lightly to be flouted. The production of the plays is thus still apt to be marked by a timid respect for 'the usual thing'; their acting is crippled by pseudo-traditions, which are inert because they are not Shakespearean at all. They are the accumulation of two centuries of progressive misconception and distortion of his playwright's art. On the other hand, England has been spared production of Shakespeare according to this or that even more irrelevant theory of presentationalism, symbolism, constructivism or what not. There is the breach in the wall of 'realism', but we have not yet made up our minds to pass through, taking our Shakespeare with us.

Incidentally, we owe the beginning of the breach to Mr William Poel, who, with fanatical courage, when 'realism' was at the tottering height of its triumph in the later revivals of Sir Henry Irving, and the yet more richly upholstered revelations of Sir Herbert Tree, thrust the Elizabethan stage in all its apparent eccentricity upon our unwilling notice.' Mr Poel shook complacency. He could not expect to do much more; for he was a logical reformer. He showed us the Elizabethan stage, with Antony and Cleopatra, Troilus and Cressida, in their ruffs and farthingales as for Shakespeare's audiences they lived. Q.E.D. There, however, as far as the popular theatre was concerned, the matter seemed to rest for twenty years or so. But it was just such a demonstration that was needed; anything less drastic and provocative might have been passed over with mild approval.

To get the balance true, let us admit that while Shakespeare was an Elizabethan playwright he was—and now is to us—predominantly something much more. Therefore we had better not too unquestioningly thrust him back within the confines his genius has escaped, nor

presume him to have felt the pettier circumstances of his
theatre sacrosanct. Nor can we turn Elizabethans as we
watch the plays; and every mental effort to do so will
subtract from our enjoyment of them. This is the case
against the circumstantial reproduction of Shakespeare's
staging. But Mr Poel's achievement remains; he cleared
for us from Shakespeare's stagecraft the scenic rubbish
by which it had been so long encumbered and disguised.
And we could now, if we would, make a promising fresh
start. For the scholars, on their side, have lately—the
scholarly among them—cut clear of the transcendental
fog (scenic illusion of another sort) in which their nineteenth-century peers loved to lose themselves, and they
too are beginning again at the beginning. A text acquires
virtue now by its claim to be a prompt book, and the
most comprehensive work of our time upon the Elizabethan stage is an elaborate sorting-out of plays, companies
and theatres. On Dr Pollard's treatment of the texts and
on the foundations of fact laid by Sir Edmund Chambers
a new scholarship is rising, aiming first to see Shakespeare in the theatre for which he wrote. It is a scholarship, therefore, by which the theatre of today can profit,
to which, by its acting of Shakespeare, it could contribute, one would hope. Nor should the scholars disdain
the help; for criticism cannot live upon criticism, it needs
refreshment from the living art. Besides, what is all the
criticism and scholarship finally for if not to keep Shakespeare alive? And he must always be most alive—even
if roughly and rudely alive—in the theatre. Let the
scholars force a way in there, if need be. Its fervid
atmosphere will do them good; the benefit will be mutual.

These Prefaces are an attempt to profit by this new
scholarship and to contribute to it some research into
Shakespeare's stagecraft, by examining the plays, one

after another, in the light of the interpretation he designed for them, so far as this can be deduced; to discover, if possible, the production he would have desired for them, all merely incidental circumstances apart. They might profit more written a generation hence, for the ground they build upon is still far from clear. And this introduction is by no means a conspectus of the subject; that can only come as a sequel. There has been, in this branch of Shakespearean study, too much generalization and far too little analysis of material.[2]

Shakespeare's Stagecraft

SHAKESPEARE'S own career was not a long one. The whole history of the theatre he wrote for does not cover a century. Between Marlowe and Massinger, from the first blaze to the glowing of the embers, it is but fifty years. Yet even while Shakespeare was at work, the stage to which he fitted his plays underwent constant and perhaps radical change. From Burbage's first theatre to the Globe, then to Blackfriars, not to mention excursions to Court and into the great halls—change of audiences and their behaviour, of their taste, development of the art of acting, change of the stage itself and its resources were all involved in the progress, and are all, we may be sure, reflected to some degree in the plays themselves. We guess at the conditions of each sort of stage and theatre, but there is often the teasing question to which of them had a play, as we have it now, been adapted. And of the 'private' theatre, most in vogue for the ten years preceding the printing of the First Folio so far we know least. The dating of texts and their ascription to the usages of a particular theatre may often be a searchlight upon their stagecraft. Here is much work for the new scholarship.

Conversely, the watchful working-out of the plays in action upon this stage or that would be of use to the scholars, who otherwise must reconstruct their theatre and gloss their texts as in a vacuum. The play was once fitted to the stage; it is by no means impossible to rebuild that stage now, with its doors, balconies, curtains and machines, by measuring the needs of the play. It is idle, for instance, to imagine scenes upon inner or upper stage without evidence that they will be audible or visible there; and editing is still vitiated by lack of this simple knowledge. Here, if nowhere else, this present research must fall short, for its method should rightly be experimental; more than one mind should be at work on it, moreover.

The text of a play is a score waiting performance, and the performance and its preparation are, almost from the beginning, a work of collaboration. A producer may direct the preparation, certainly. But if he only knows how to give orders, he has mistaken his vocation; he had better be a drill-sergeant. He might talk to his company when they all met together for the first time to study *Love's Labour's Lost*, *Julius Cæsar* or *King Lear*, on some such lines as these Prefaces pursue, giving a considered opinion of the play, drawing a picture of it in action, providing, in fact, a hypothesis which mutual study would prove—and might partly disprove. No sort of study of a play can better the preparation of its performance if this is rightly done. The matured art of the playwright lies in giving life to characters in action, and the secret of it in giving each character a due chance in the battle, the action of a play becoming literally the fighting of a battle of character. So the greater the playwright, the wider and deeper his sympathies, the more genuine this opposition will be and the less easily will a single mind grasp it, as it must be grasped, in the fullness of its emotion. The dialogue of a play runs—and often intricately—upon lines of reason, but it is charged besides with an emotion which speech releases, yet only releases fully when the speaker is—as an actor is—identified with the character. There is further the incidental action, implicit in the dialogue, which springs to life only when a scene is in being. A play, in fact, as we find it written, is a magic spell; and even the magician cannot always foresee the full effect of it.

Not every play, it must be owned, will respond to such intensive study. Many, ambitiously conceived, would collapse under the strain. Many are mere occasions for display of their actors' wit or eloquence, good looks or nice behaviour, and meant to be no more; and if they are skilfully contrived the parts fit together and the whole machine should go like clockwork. Nor, in fact, are even the greatest plays often so studied. There is hardly a theatre in the world where masterpiece and trumpery alike are not rushed through rehearsals to an arbitrarily effective performance, little more learned of them than the words, gaps in the understanding of them filled up with 'business'—effect without cause, the demand for this being the curse of the theatre as of other arts, as of other things than art. Not to such treatment will the greater plays of Shakespeare yield their secrets. But working upon a stage which reproduced the essential conditions of his, working as students, not as showmen merely, a company of actors might well find many of the riddles of the library answering themselves unasked. And these Prefaces could best be a record of such work, if such work were to be done.

We cannot, on the other hand, begin our research by postulating the principles of the Elizabethan stage. One is tempted to say it had none, was too much a child of nature to bother about such things. Principles were doubtless imposed upon it when it reached respectability, and heads would be bowed to the yoke. Shakespeare's among them? He had served a most practical apprenticeship to his trade. If he did not hold horses at the door, he sat behind the curtains, we may be sure, and held the prompt book on occasion. He acted, he cobbled other men's plays, he could write his own to order. Such a one may stay a journeyman if he is not a genius, but he will not become a doctrinaire. Shakespeare's work shows such principles as the growth of a tree shows. It is not haphazard merely because it is not formal; it is shaped by inner strength. The theatre, as he found it, allowed him and encouraged him to great freedom of development. Because the material resources of a stage are simple, it does not follow that the technique of its playwriting will stay so. Crude work may show up more crudely, when there are none of the fal-lals of illusion to disguise it that the modern theatre provides. But, if he has it in him, a dramatist can, so unfettered, develop the essentials of his art more boldly and more subtly too. The Elizabethan drama made an amazingly quick advance from crudity to an excellence which was often technically most elaborate. The advance and the not less amazing gulf which divides its best from its worst may be ascribed to the simplicity of the machinery it employed. That its decadence was precipitated by the influence of the Masque and the shifting of its centre of interest from the barer public stage to the candle-lit private theatre, where the machinery of the Masque became effective, it would be rash to assert; but the occurrences are suspiciously related. Man and machine (here at any rate is a postulate, if a platitude!) are false allies in the theatre, secretly at odds; and when man gets the worst of it, drama is impoverished; and the struggle, we may add, is perennial. No great drama depends upon pageantry. All great drama tends to concentrate upon character; and, even so, not upon picturing men as they show themselves to the world like figures on a stage—though that is how it must ostensibly show them—but on the hidden man. And the progress of Shakespeare's art from *Love's Labour's Lost* to *Hamlet,* and thereafter with a difference, lies in the simplifying of this paradox and the solving of the problem it presents; and the process involves the developing of a very subtle sort of stagecraft indeed.

For one result we have what we may call a very self-contained drama. Its chief values, as we know, have not changed with the fashions of the theatre. It relies much on the music of the spoken word, and a company of schoolchildren with pleasant voices, and an ear for rhythm, may vociferate through a play to some effect. It is as much to be enjoyed in the reading, if we hear it in imagination as we read, as drama meant to be acted can be. As with its simplicities then, so it should be, we presume, with its complexities. The subtly emotional use of verse and the interplay of motive and character, can these not be appreciated apart from the bare boards of their original setting? It does not follow. It neither follows that the advantages of the Elizabethan stage were wholly negative nor that, with our present knowledge, we can imagine the full effect of a play in action upon it. The imagining of a play in action is, under no circumstances, an easy thing.[3] What would one not give to go backward through the centuries to see the first performance of *Hamlet,* played as Shakespeare had it played![4] In default, if we could but make ourselves read it as if it were a manuscript fresh from its author's hands! There is much to be said for turning one's back on the editors, even, when possible, upon the First Folio with its demarcation of acts and scenes, in favour of the Quartos—Dr Pollard's 'good' Quartos—in their yet greater simplicity.

The Convention of Place

IT is, for instance, hard to discount the impression made merely by reading: *Scene i—Elsinore. A platform before the Castle*; and most of us have, to boot, early memories of painted battlements and tenth-century castles (of ageing Hamlets and their portly mothers for that matter) very difficult to dismiss. No great harm, one protests; it was a help, perhaps, to the unimaginative. But it is a first step to the certain misunderstanding of Shakespeare's stagecraft. The 'if, how and when' of the presenting of localities on the Elizabethan stage is, of course, a complex question. Shakespeare himself seems to have followed, consciously, no principles in the matter, nor was his practice very logical, nor at all consistent. It may vary with the play he is writing and the particular stage he is writing for; it will best be studied in relation to each play. We can, however, free ourselves from one general misconception which belongs to our own over-logical standpoint. When we learn with a shock of surprise—having begun in the schoolroom upon the Shakespeare of the editors, it comes as belated news to us—that neither battlements, throne rooms nor picturesque churchyards were to be seen at the Globe, and that *Elsinore. A platform before the Castle* is not Shakespeare at all, we yet imagine ourselves among the audience there busily conjuring these things up before the eye of faith. The Elizabethan audience was at no such pains. Nor was this their alternative to seeing the actors undisguisedly concerned with the doors, curtains and balconies which, by the play's requirements, should have been anything but what they were. As we, when a play has no hold on us, may fall to thinking about the scenery, so to a Globe audience, unmoved, the stage might be an obvious bare stage. But are we conscious of the scenery behind the actor when the play really moves us? If we are, there is something very wrong with the scenery, which should know its place as a background. The audience was not conscious of curtain and balcony when Burbage played Hamlet to them. They were conscious of Hamlet. That conventional background faded as does our painted illusion, and they certainly did not deliberately conjure up in its place mental pictures of Elsinore. The genus audience is passive, if expectant, imaginatively lazy till roused, never, one may be sure, at pains to make any effort that is generally unnecessary to enjoyment.

With Shakespeare the locality of a scene has dramatic importance, or it has none; and this is as true of his early plays as his late ones. Both in *Richard II* and *Antony and Cleopatra*, scene after scene passes with no exact indication of where we may be. With *Cleopatra* we are surely in Egypt, with Cæsar in Rome. Pompey appears, and the talk tells us that both Egypt and Rome are elsewhere; but positively where Pompey is at the moment we never learn.[5] Indoors or outdoors? The action of the scene or the clothing of the characters will tell us this if we need to know. But, suddenly transported to the Parthian war, our whereabouts is made amply plain. It is, however, made plain by allusion. The information peeps out through talk of kindred things; we are hardly aware we are being told, and, again, we learn no more than we need to learn. This, truly, is a striking development from the plump and plain

> Barkloughly Castle call they this at hand?

of Richard II, even from the more descriptive

> I am a stranger here in Gloucestershire:
> These high wild hills and rough, uneven ways
> Draw out our miles. . .

by which Shakespeare pictures and localizes the manoeuvres of Richard and Bolingbroke when he wants to.
But the purpose is the same, and the method essentially
the same.[6] Towards the end of the later play come scene
after scene of the marching and countermarching of
armies, of fighting, of truce, all the happenings of three
days' battle. Acts III and IV contain twenty-eight scenes
long and short; some of them are very short; three of
them have but four lines apiece. The editors conscien-
tiously ticket them *A plain near Actium, Another part of the
plain, Another part of the plain* and so on, and conclude that
Shakespeare is really going too far and too fast, is indeed
(I quote Sir Edmund Chambers) 'in some danger of
outrunning the apprehensions of his auditory.' Indeed he
might be if this cinematographic view of his intentions
were the right one! But it utterly falsifies them. Show an
audience such a succession of painted scenes—if you
could at the pace required—and they would give attention to nothing else whatever; the drama would pass
unnoticed. Had Shakespeare tried to define the whereabouts of every scene in any but the baldest phrases—the
protesting editors seem not to see that he makes no
attempt to; only *they* do!—he would have had to lengthen
and complicate them; had he written only a labelling
line or two he would still have distracted his audience
from the essential drama. Ignoring whereabouts, letting
it at most transpire when it naturally will, the characters
capture all attention. This is the true gain of the bare
stage; unless to some dramatic end no precious words
need be spent, in complying with the undramatic demands of space and time; incarnation of character can
be all in all. Given such a crisis as this the gain is yet
greater. We are carried through the phases of the three
days' battle; and what other stage convention would
allow us so varied a view of it, could so isolate the true

drama of it? For do we not pass through such a crisis in reality with just that indifference to time and place? These scenes, in their kind, show Shakespeare's stage-craft, not at its most reckless, but at its very best, and exemplify perfectly the freedom he enjoyed that the stage of visual illusion has inevitably lost. His drama is attached solely to its actors and their acting; that, perhaps, puts it in a phrase. They carry place and time with them as they move. The modern theatre still accepts the convention that measures time more or less by a play's convenience; a half-hour stands for an hour or more, and we never question the vagary. It was no more strange to an Elizabethan audience to see a street in Rome turned, in the use made of it, to the Senate House by the drawing of a curtain and the disclosure of Cæsar's state, to find Cleopatra's Monument now on the upper stage because Antony had to be drawn up to it, later on the lower because Cleopatra's death-scene could best be played there; it would seem that they were not too astonished even when Juliet, having taken leave of Romeo on the balcony of her bedroom and watched him descend to the lower stage, the scene continuing, came down, a few lines later, to the lower stage herself, bringing, so to speak, her bedroom with her—since this apparently is what she must have done.[7] For neither Senate House, Monument nor balcony had rights and reality of their own. They existed for the convenience of the actors, whose touch gave them life, a shadowy life at most; neglected, they existed no longer.[8]

Shakespeare's stagecraft concentrates, and inevitably, upon opportunity for the actor. We think now of the plays themselves; their first public knew them by their acting; and the development of the actor's art from the agilities and funniments of the clown, and from round-mouthed rhetoric to imaginative interpreting of character by such standards as Hamlet set up for his players, was a factor in the drama's triumph that we now too often ignore. Shakespeare himself, intent more and more upon plucking out the heart of the human mystery, stimulated his actors to a poignancy and intimacy of emotional expression—still can stimulate them to it—as no other playwright has quite learned to do.

The Speaking of the Verse

His verse was, of course, his chief means to this emotional expression; and when it comes to staging the plays, the speaking of verse must be the foundation of all study. The changes of three hundred years have of themselves put difficulties in our way here; though there are some besides—as one imagines—of Shakespeare's own making. Surely his syntax must now and then have puzzled even his contemporaries. Could they have made much more than we can of Leontes'

> Affection! thy intention stabs the centre;
> Thou dost make possible things not so held,
> Communicat'st with dreams;—How can this be?
> With what's unreal thou coactive art,
> And fellow'st nothing; then, 'tis very credent
> Thou may'st co-join with something; and thou dost;
> And that beyond commission; and I find it,
> And that to the infection of my brains,
> And hardening of my brows.

The confusion of thought and intricacy of language is dramatically justified. Shakespeare is picturing a genuinely jealous man (the sort of man that Othello was *not*) in the grip of a mental epilepsy. We parse the passage and dispute its sense; spoken, as it was meant to be, in a choking torrent of passion, probably a modicum of sense slipped through, and its first hearers did not find it a mere rigmarole. But we are apt to miss even that much. Other passages, of early and late writing, may always have had as much sound as sense to them; but now, to the casual hearer, they will convey more sound than sense by far. Nor do puns mean to us what they meant to the Elizabethans, delighting in their language for its own sake. Juliet's tragic fantasia upon 'Aye' and 'I' sounds all but ridiculous, and one sympathizes with an actress hesitating to venture on it. How far, apart from the shifting of accents and the recolouring of vowels, has not the whole habit of English speech changed in these three hundred years? In the theatre it was slowing down, one fancies, throughout the eighteenth century; and in the nineteenth, as far as Shakespeare was concerned, it grew slower and slower, till on occasions one thought—even hoped—that shortly the actor would stop altogether. There may have been more than one cause; imitation of the French Augustans, the effort to make antiquated phrases understood, the increasing size of the theatres themselves would all contribute to it. The result, in any case, is disastrous. Elizabethan drama was built upon vigour and beauty of speech. The groundlings may often have deserved Shakespeare's strictures, but they would stand in discomfort for an hour or so to be stirred by the sound of verse. Some of the actors no doubt were robustious periwig-pated fellows, but, equally, it was no empty ideal of acting he put into Hamlet's mouth—and Burbage's. We may suppose that at its best the mere speaking of the plays was a very brilliant thing, compared to *bel canto*, or to a pianist's virtuosity. The emotional appeal of our modern music was in it, and it could be tested by ears trained to the rich and delicate fretwork of the music of that day. Most Hamlets—not being playwrights—make a mild joke of telling us they'd as lief the town-crier spoke their lines, but we may hear in it the echo of some of Shakespeare's sorest trials.

The speaking of his verse must be studied, of course, in relation to the verse's own development. The actor must not attack its supple complexities in *Antony and Cleopatra* and *Cymbeline*, the mysterious dynamics of *Macbeth*, the nobilities of *Othello*, its final pastoral simplicities in *A Winter's Tale* and *The Tempest* without preliminary training in the lyricism, the swift brilliance and the masculine clarity of the earlier plays. A modern actor, alas, thinks it simple enough to make his way, splay-footed, through

The cloud-capped towers, the gorgeous palaces...

though Berowne's

I, forsooth, in love...

or one of Oberon's apostrophes will defeat him utterly. And, without an ear trained to the delicacy of the earlier work, his hearers, for their part, will never know how shamefully he is betraying the superb ease of the later. If we are to make Shakespeare our own again we must all be put to a little trouble about it. We must recapture as far as may be his lost meanings; and the sense of a phrase we *can* recapture, though instinctive emotional response to it may be a loss forever. The tunes that he writes to, the whole great art of his music-making, we can master. Actors can train their ears and tongues and can train our ears to it. We talk of lost arts. No art is ever lost while the means to it survive. Our faculties rust by disuse and by misuse are coarsened, but they quickly recover delight in a beautiful thing. Here, at any rate, is the touchstone by which all interpreting of Shakespeare the playwright must first—and last—be tried.

The Boy-Actress

MORE than one of the conditions of his theatre made this medium of accomplished speech of such worth to him. Boys played the women parts; and what could a boy bring to Juliet, Rosalind or Cleopatra beyond grace of manner and charm of speech? We have been used to women on the stage for two hundred and fifty years or more, and a boy Juliet—if the name on the programme revealed one, for nothing else might—would seem an odd fish to us; no one would risk a squeaking Cleopatra; though, as for Rosalind, through three-parts of the play a boy would have the best of it. But the parts were written for boys; not, therefore, without consideration of how boys could act them most convincingly. Hence, of course, the popularity of the heroine so disguised. The disguise was perfect; the make-believe one degree more complex, certainly, than it needs to be with us; but once you start make-believe it matters little how far you go with it; there is, indeed, some enjoyment in the make-believe itself. But, further, it is Shakespeare's constant care to demand nothing of a boy-actress that might turn to unseemliness or ridicule. He had not much taste for what is called 'domestic drama,' nor does he dose us very heavily with Doll Tearsheet, Mistress Overdone and their like. Constance mourns Arthur's loss, Lady Macduff has her little son, but no mother croons over the child in her arms. Paulina brings Hermione's baby to Leontes, it is true; but see with what tact, from this point of view, the episode is managed. And love-scenes are most carefully contrived. Romeo and Juliet are seldom alone together; never for long, but in the balcony-scene; and in this, the most famous of love-scenes, they are kept from all contact with each other. Consider *Antony and*

Cleopatra. Here is a tragedy of sex without one single scene of sexual appeal. That aspect of Cleopatra is reflected for us in talk about her; mainly by Enobarbus, who is not mealymouthed; but his famed description of her voluptuousness is given us when she has been out of our sight for several scenes. The play opens with her parting from Antony, and in their two short encounters we see her swaying him by wit, malice and with the moods of her mind. Not till the story takes its tragic plunge and sex is drowned in deeper passion are they ever intimately together; till he is brought to her dying there has been occasion for but one embrace. Contrast this with a possible Cleopatra planned to the advantage of the actress of today.

Shakespeare, artist that he was, turned this limitation to account, made loss into a gain.[9] Feminine charm—of which the modern stage makes such capital—was a medium denied him. So his men and women encounter upon a plane where their relation is made rarer and intenser by poetry, or enfranchised in a humour which surpasses more primitive love-making. And thus, perhaps, he was helped to discover that the true stuff of tragedy and of the liveliest comedy lies beyond sensual bounds. His studies of women seem often to be begun from some spiritual paces beyond the point at which a modern dramatist leaves off. Curious that not a little of the praise lavished upon the beauty and truth of them— mainly by women—may be due to their having been written to be played by boys!

Much could be said for the restoring of the celibate stage; but the argument, one fears, would be academic. Here, though, is practical counsel. Let the usurping actress remember that her sex is a liability, not an asset. The dramatist of today may refuse to exploit its allure- ments, but may legitimately allow for the sympathetic effect of it; though the less he does so, perhaps, the better for his play and the more gratitude the better sort of actress will show him. But Shakespeare makes no such demands, has left no blank spaces for her to fill with her charm. He asks instead for self-forgetful clarity of perception, and for a sensitive, spirited, athletic beauty of speech and conduct, which will leave prettiness and its lures at a loss, and the crudities of more Circean appeal looking very crude indeed.

The Soliloquy

THIS convention of the boy-actress may be said to give a certain remoteness to a play's acting. The soliloquy brings a compensating intimacy, and its use was an important part of Shakespeare's stagecraft. Its recognized usefulness was for the disclosing of the plot, but he soon improved upon this. Soliloquy becomes the means by which he brings us not only to a knowledge of the more secret thoughts of his characters, but into the closest emotional touch with them too. Here the platform stage helped him, as the stage of scenic illusion now defeats his purpose. But it is not altogether a question of 'realism' and the supposed obligation this lays upon a real man in a real-looking room to do nothing he would not do if the whole affair were real.

There is no escape from convention in the theatre, and all conventions can be made acceptable, though they cannot all be used indiscriminately, for they are founded in the physical conditions of the stage of their origin and are often interdependent one with another. Together they form a code, and they are as a treaty made with the audience. No article of it is to be abrogated unless we can be persuaded to consent, and upon its basis we surrender our imaginations to the playwright.

With the soliloquy upon the platform stage it is a case—as so often where convention is concerned—of extremes meeting. There is no illusion, so there is every illusion. Nothing very strange about this man, not even the dress he wears, leaning forward a little we could touch him; we are as intimate and familiar with him as it is possible to be. We agree to call him 'Hamlet', to suppose that he is where he says he is, we admit that he thinks aloud and in blank verse too. It is possible that the more we are asked to imagine the easier we find it to do. It is certain that, once our imagination is working, visual illusion will count for little in the stimulating of emotion beside this intimacy that allows the magnetism of personality full play.

There is no more important task for the producer of Shakespeare than to restore to the soliloquy its rightful place in a play's economy, and in particular to regain for it full emotional effect. We now accept the convention frigidly, the actor manoeuvres with it timidly. Banished behind footlights into that other world of illusion, the solitary self-communing figure rouses our curiosity at best. Yet further adapted to the self-contained methods of modern acting, the soliloquy has quite inevitably become a slack link in the play's action, when it should be a recurring reinforcement to its strength. Shakespeare never pinned so many dramatic fortunes to a merely utilitarian device. Time and again he may be feeling his way through a scene for a grip on his audience, and it is the soliloquy ending it that will give him—and his actor—the stranglehold. When he wishes to quicken the pulse of the action, to screw up its tension in a second or so, the soliloquy serves him well. For a parallel to its full effectiveness on Shakespeare's stage we should really look to the modern music-hall comedian getting on terms with his audience. We may measure the response to Burbage's

O, that this too too solid flesh would melt . . .

by recalling—those of us that happily can—Dan Leno
as a washerwoman, confiding domestic troubles to a
theatre full of friends, and taken unhindered to their
hearts. The problem is not really a difficult one. If we
solve the physical side of it by restoring, in essentials,
the relation between actor and audience that the intimacy of the platform stage provided, the rest should soon
solve itself.

Costume

THE problem of costume, when it arises, is a subtler one;
nor probably is it capable of any logical solution. Half
the plays can be quite appropriately dressed in the
costume of Shakespeare's own time. It is a false logic
which suggests that to match their first staging we should
dress them in the costume of ours. For with costume
goes custom and manners—or the lack of them. It may
be both a purge and a tonic to the sluggish-fancied
spectator to be shown a Prince of Denmark in coat and
trousers and a Grave-digger in a bowler hat, for remin-
der that here is a play, not a collection of ritualized
quotations. But physic is for the sick; also, there may be
less drastic cures. When archaeology took hold upon the
nineteenth-century mind it became a matter of moment
to lodge Hamlet in historic surroundings; and withers
were wrung by the anachronisms of ducats and a murder
of Gonzago, French rapiers and the rest. A needlessly
teasing difficulty; why reproduce it in terms of a young
man in a dinner jacket searching for a sword—a thing
not likely to be lying about in his modern mother's sitting
room—with which to kill Polonius, who certainly has
window curtains to hide behind instead of arras? This

gain of intimacy—with a Hamlet we might find sitting opposite at a dinner party—may well be a gain in sympathy. It was originally a great gain, a gift to Shakespeare's audience. But we pay too high a price for it.

What was the actual Elizabethan practice in this matter of costuming is not comprehensively known. We can only say safely that, as with other matters, it was neither constant, consistent, nor, from our present point of view, rational. It was based upon the use of the clothes of the time; but these might be freely and fantastically adapted to suit a particular play or advantage some character in it. Dramatic effect was probably the first consideration and the last. There were such fancy dresses as Oberon or Puck or Caliban might wear; there was always the symbolizing of royalty, and a king would wear a crown whenever he could; there was the utility of knowing Romans from Britons by sight in *Cymbeline*, the martial Roman from the effete Egyptian in *Antony and Cleopatra*, and a Scottish lord when you saw him in *Macbeth*, if we may judge by Malcolm's comment upon Rosse's appearance:

> My countryman; and yet I know him not.

Our difficulty, of course, arises mainly over the historical plays. Not over the English Histories, even so; we can dress Richard III or Henry V by the light of our own superior knowledge of what they wore, and never find it clash violently with anything Shakespeare has put on their backs or in their mouths. But when we come to Julius Cæsar plucking open his doublet, to the conspirators against him with their hats about their ears, and to Cleopatra's

> Cut my lace, Charmian.

not to mention British Imogen in her doublet and hose, we must stop and consider.

The common practice is, in these instances, to ignore the details of Shakespeare's text altogether; to dress Cæsar in his toga, Cleopatra in her habit as she lived, with never a stay-lace about her (though, truly, the costumier, let alone, will tend to get his fashion a few thousand years wrong and turn her out more like the wife of Tutankhamen); and as to Imogen and her surroundings, we do our best to compromise with skins and woad. This may be a lesser evil than presenting a Cæsar recalling Sir Walter Raleigh and a Cleopatra who would make us think of Mary Queen of Scots, but it is no solution of the problem. For the actors have to speak these lines, and if action and appearance contradict them, credibility is destroyed. And the constant credibility of the actor must be a producer's first care. Nor is this all, nor is it, perhaps, the most important thing to consider. The plays are full of reference, direct and indirect, to Elizabethan custom. They are, further, impregnated with what we call 'Renaissance feeling', some more, some less, but all to a degree. Now of this last we have a sense which is likelier to be a better help to their appreciation than any newfangled knowledge of the correct cut of Cleopatra's clothes will be! We know Iago for a Machiavellian figure (so called), and miss none of Shakespeare's intention. But if ever two men breathed the air of a sixteenth-century court, Hamlet and Claudius of Denmark do, and to relate them in habit and behaviour to the twilight figures of Saxo Grammaticus is as much a misinterpretation as any mauling of the text can be. They exist essentially doubtless—as do all the major characters of the plays—in their perennial humanity. But never let us forget the means by which this deeper truth of them is made vivid and actual. There have been better intellects than Shakespeare's, and poetry as good as his. He holds his supreme place by his dramatist's necessary power of bringing thought and vague emotion to the terms of action and convincing speech; further, and far more than is often allowed, by his peculiar gift of bringing into contribution the common-place traffic of life. However wide the spoken word may range, there must be the actor, anchored to the stage. However high, then, with Shakespeare, the thought or emotion may soar, we shall always find the transcendental set in the familiar. He keeps this balance constantly adjusted; and, at his play's greatest moments, when he must make most sure of our response, he will employ the simplest means. The higher arguments of the plays are thus kept always within range, and their rooted humanity blossoms in a fertile upspringing of expressive little things. Neglect or misinterpret these, the inner wealth of Shakespeare will remain, no doubt, and we may mine for it, but we shall have levelled his landscape bare.

Shakespeare's own attitude in this matter of costume and customs was as inconsistent as his practice was casual. He knew what *his* Cæsar or Cleopatra would be wearing and would casually drop in a reference to it. Yet the great Romans themselves were aliens to him. The great idea of Rome fired his imagination. Brutus, Cassius and Antony do not turn typical Elizabethan gentlemen; and to the end of that play he is striving to translate Plutarch. Whenever, on the other hand, even for a moment he has made a character all his own, he cannot but clothe it in lively familiar detail. Cleopatra's are the coquetries of a great lady of his own time, in their phrasing, in the savour. When the heights of the tragedy have to be scaled, manners will not so much matter. But if we make her, at the play's beginning, a pseudo-classic, languishing Oriental, we must do it in spite of Shakespeare, not by his help. What then is the solution of this problem, if the sight of the serpent of old Nile in a farthingale will too dreadfully offend us? We can compromise. Look at Tintoretto's and Paolo Veronese's paintings of 'classic' subjects. We accept them readily enough.

Sometimes, within the boundaries of a play, the centuries seem all at odds. *Cymbeline* need not trouble us, its Roman Britain is pure 'once upon a time'. But in *King Lear*, for instance, Shakespeare is at unwonted pains to throw us back into some heathen past. Yet Edmund is another Iago, Edgar might have been at Wittenberg with Hamlet, and Oswald steps straight from the seventeenth-century London streets. Here, though, the dominant barbarism is the important thing; the setting for Goneril and Regan, Lear's tyranny and madness, and Gloucester's blinding. To a seventeenth-century audience Oswald was so identifiable a figure that it would not matter greatly how he dressed; the modern designer of costume must show him up as best he may. Each play, in fine, if it presents a problem at all, presents its own.

The Integrity of the Text

THE text, one says at first blush, can present no problem at all. The plays should be acted as Shakespeare wrote them—how dispute it? They should be; and it is as well, before we discuss hard cases, to have the principle freely admitted. Lip service enough is done it nowadays, and Colley Cibber's *Richard III*, Tate's *Lear* and Garrick's improvements are at the back of our bookshelves, but we still find Messrs John Doe and Richard Roe slicing out lines by the dozen and even a scene or so, or chopping and changing them to suit their scenery. This will not do. Shakespeare was not a perfect playwright; there can be no such thing. Nor did he aim at a mechanical perfection, but a vitality, and this he achieved. At best then, we cut and carve the body of a play to its peril. It may be robustly, but it may be very delicately organized. And we still know little enough of the laws of its existence, and some of us, perhaps, are not such very skilful surgeons; nor is any surgeon to be recommended who operates for his own convenience.

This good rule laid down, what are the exceptions that go to prove it? There is the pornographic difficulty. This is not such a stumbling block to us as it was to Bowdler, to some bright young eyes nowadays it is quite imperceptible, in fact. Yet, saving their presence, it exists; for it exists aesthetically. Shakespeare's characters often make obscene jokes. The manners of his time permitted it. The public manners of ours still do not. Now the dramatic value of a joke is to be measured by its effect upon an audience, and each is meant to make its own sort of effect. If then, instead of giving them a passing moment's amusement, it makes a thousand people uncomfortable and for the next five minutes very self-conscious, it fails of its true effect. This argument must not be stretched to cover the silliness of turning 'God' into 'Heaven' and of making Othello call Desdemona a 'wanton' (the practice, as I recollect, of the eighteen-nineties), nor to such deodorizing of *Measure for Measure* that it becomes hard to discover what all the fuss is about. If an audience cannot think of Angelo and the Duke, Pompey and Lucio, Isabella and Mistress Overdone, and themselves to boot, as fellow-creatures all, the play is not for them. Othello must call Desdemona a 'whore', and let those that do not like it leave the theatre; what have such queasy minds to do with the pity and terror of her murder and his death? Again, to make Beatrice so mealymouthed that she may not tell us how the devil is to meet her at the gates of hell, 'like an old cuckold with horns on his head', is to dress her in a crinoline, not a farthingale. But suppression of a few of the more scabrous jokes will not leave a play much the poorer; nor, one may add, will the average playgoer be much the wiser or merrier for hearing them, since they are often quite hard to understand.

Topical passages are a similar difficulty. With their savour, if not their very meaning lost, they show like dead wood in the living tree of the dialogue and are better, one would suppose, cut away. But no hard and fast rule will apply. Macbeth's porter's farmer and equivocator will never win spontaneous laughter again. But we cannot away with them, or nothing is left of the porter. Still the baffled low comedian must not, as his wont is, obscure the lines with bibulous antics. There will be that little dead spot in the play, and nothing can be done about it. Rosencrantz' reference to the 'eyrie of children' is meaningless except to the student. Is the play the poorer for the loss of it? But the logic that will take this out had better not rob us of

> Dead shepherd, now I find thy saw of might;
> Who ever loved that loved not at first sight?

And there is the strange case of

The lady of the Strachy married the yeoman of the wardrobe.

Nobody knows what it means, but everybody finds it funny when it is spoken in its place. And this has its parallels.

In general, however, better play the plays as we find them. The blue pencil is a dangerous weapon; and its use grows on a man, for it solves too many little difficulties far too easily.

Lastly, for a golden rule, whether staging or costuming or cutting is in question, and a comprehensive creed, a producer might well pin this on his wall: Gain Shakespeare's effects by Shakespeare's means when you can; for, plainly, this will be the better way. But gain Shakespeare's effects; and it is your business to discern them.

1927

Notes

1 But it should not be forgotten that Sir Herbert Tree, happy in the orthodoxy of public favour, welcomed the heretic Mr Poel more than once to a share in his Shakespeare Festivals.

2 I do not deal in general therefore with certain vexed questions, such as act-division, which still need to be looked at, I think, in the light of the particular play.

3 I remember a most intelligent reader of a modern play missing the whole point of a scene through which the chief character was to sit conspicuously and eloquently silent. He counted only with the written dialogue. I remember, when I thought I knew *King Lear* well enough, being amazed at the effect, all dialogue apart, of the mere meeting, when I saw it, of blind Gloucester and mad Lear.

4 Though, in a sense, there was no first performance of *Hamlet*. And doubtless many of the audience for Shakespeare's new version of the old play only thought he had spoiled a good story of murder and revenge by adding too much talk to it.

5 Unless it may be said that we learn in the scene after whereabouts he *was*.

6 And in *Coriolanus*, which probably postdates *Antony and Cleopatra*, with Marcius' 'A goodly city is this Antium,' we are back to the barely informative. It serves Shakespeare's purpose; he asks no more.

7 I fancy, though, that the later Shakespeare would have thought this a clumsy device.

8 How far this is true of other dramatists than Shakespeare I do not pretend to say; nor how far, with him, the influence of the private theatre, making undoubtedly towards the scenic stage

and (much later) for illusion, did not modify his practice, when he had that stage to consider. A question, again, for the bibliographers and historians.

9 There is no evidence, of course, that he felt it a loss, no such reference to the insufficiency of the boy-actress as there is to the overself-sufficiency of the clown. Women did appear in the Masques, if only to dance, so the gulf to be bridged was not a broad one. But the Elizabethan was as shocked by the notion of women appearing upon the public stage as the Chinese playgoer is today.

Love's Labour's Lost

HERE is a fashionable play; now, by three hundred years, out of fashion. Nor did it ever, one supposes, make a very wide appeal. It abounds in jokes for the elect. Were you not numbered among them you laughed, for safety, in the likeliest places. A year or two later the elect themselves might be hard put to it to remember what the joke was.

The Producer's Problem

WERE this all one could say of *Love's Labour's Lost*, the question of its staging today—with which we are first and last concerned—would be quickly answered, and Lose No Labour here be the soundest advice. For spontaneous enjoyment is the life of the theatre. If a performance must be accompanied by a lecture, if, for instance, when Holofernes is at the point of

Bone, bone for benè: Priscian a little scratched. 'Twill serve.

we need his modern exemplar in cap and gown, standing on one side of the proscenium, to interrupt with 'One moment, please! The allusion here, if you wish to appreciate its humour, is to ... '; or if he must warn us, 'In the next scene, ladies and gentlemen, you will notice a reference to the charge-house on the top of the mountain. This is thought by the best authorities to denote ... ' not much fun will survive. For a glossary in the programme something might be said, even for a preliminary lecture. No; this last, one fears, would leave the actors with too hard a task turning classroom back to theatre. Half-digested information lies a little heavily on one's sense of humour.

It is true that with no play three hundred years old can we press our 'spontaneous' too hard. For the full appreciation of anything in Shakespeare some knowledge is asked of its why and wherefore. Hamlet and Falstaff however, Rosalind and Imogen, are compact of qualities which fashion cannot change; the barriers of dramatic convention, strange habits, tricks of speech are of small enough account with them. But what is back of these word-gymnastics of Rosaline and Berowne, Holofernes' jargon, Armado's antics? The play is a satire, a comedy of affectations. The gymnastics, the jargon and the antics are the fun. Yet a play hardly lives by such brilliancies alone. While the humour of them is fresh and holds our attention, actors may lend it a semblance of life; for there at least *they* are, alive in their kind! No play, certainly, can count on survival if it strikes no deeper root nor bears more perennial flowers. If its topical brilliance were all, Shakespeare's name tagged to this one would keep it a place on the scholar's dissecting table; in the theatre *Love's Labour's Lost* would be dead, past all question. But there is life in it. The satire beside, Shakespeare the poet had his fling. It abounds in beauties of fancy and phrase, as beautiful today as ever. We find in it Shakespeare the dramatist learning his art. To students the most interesting thing about the play is the evidence of this; of the trial and error, his discovery of fruitful soil and fruitless. The producer, pledged to present an audience with a complete something, cannot, of course, be content with promise and experiment. Measuring this early Shakespeare by the later, we may as well own there is not much more. But the root of the matter is already in him; he is the dramatist born, and all, or nearly all, is at least instinct with dramatic life. It is oftenest his calculations and his cleverness that betray him.

For satire and no more is too apt to prove dramatically

fruitless. A play's values are human values, and a playwright's first task is to give his creatures being. Imaginative love for them may help him to; even hate may; but a mocking detachment cannot. If he is to shoot at their follies he must yet build up the target first; and if it is not a convincing one there will be little credit in the shooting. He cannot, of course, in a play, take direct aim himself, unless he use the method of the Moralities or its like. There is the less direct method of twisting a set of familiar heroic figures awry. Shakespeare made this experiment, not too successfully, in *Troilus and Cressida*. But his obvious plan will be to turn one or more of his creatures satirists themselves, and under their cover plant his own shafts. Even so, he must give the victims their chance, or the play will be lopsided and come tumbling down.

The Shakespeare who sets out to write *Love's Labour's Lost* is a very clever young man, a wit, a sonneteer. He is 'in the movement'. He flatters his admirers by excelling in the things they admire; he will flatter his rivals hardly less by this attention he means to pay them. But your clever young man is usually more than a little impressed by the things he mocks at; he mocks at them in self-defence, it may be, lest they impress him too much. Mockery is apt, indeed, to capitulate to the thing mocked, to be absorbed by it. And these academic follies of Navarre, the fantastic folly of Armado, the pedantic folly of schoolmaster and parson—sometimes the satire is so fine that the folly seems the clever young man's own. Yet this weakness of the would-be satirist is the budding dramatist's strength. Shakespeare cannot resist his creatures; he never quite learned to. He cannot make mere targets of them. He cannot resist his own genius, poetic or dramatic; all through the play we find the leaven of it working.

He has not written ten lines before the poet in him breaks bounds. Is this the voice of that frigid wiseacre Navarre; does this suggest the 'little academe'?

> Therefore, brave conquerors—for so you are,
> That war against your own affections
> And the huge army of the world's desires . . .

But the clever young man recollects himself; and here, soon enough, is the sort of thing he has set out to write.

KING.   How well he's read, to reason against reading!
DUMAIN.   Proceeded well, to stop all good proceeding!
LONGAVILLE. He weeds the corn, and still lets grow the
weeding.
BEROWNE.   The spring is near, when green geese are
a-breeding.
DUMAIN.   How follows that?
BEROWNE.   Fit in his place and time.
DUMAIN.   In reason nothing.
BEROWNE.   Something then in rhyme .

Pretty tricksy stuff! Well enough done to show that he quite enjoyed doing it, but the sort of thing that almost anyone could learn to do. No signpost on the road to *Hamlet*, certainly.

But mark the dramatist in his provision at the outset of the conflict and balance that every play needs, in the setting of Berowne against his companions, one man's common sense against the crowding affectations (a sporting conflict), an ounce of reality for counterweight to a ton of shams (an instructive balance). Here also, for the moralist-critic, is the play's moral issue defined at the outset; but let us not suppose Shakespeare to have been oppressed by this. Despite his present-day idolaters he was probably not high-purposed from his cradle; moreover, he is likely to have gained most of his knowledge of life by writing plays about it. That is not a provocative paradox, but a key to the mind and method of the artist. Time and again Shakespeare tells us that he sees the world as a stage. He would not think that a belittling comparison; he takes his art too seriously. Not portentously, but as simply seriously as any man will take his purpose in life when he is lucky enough to be sure of it. We all need some centre of experience to argue from, if the world beyond our experience is to have any meaning for us. The artist transforms and multiplies experience by imagination, and may even come to think that what is true of his art will be true of the world it mirrors. This sounds absurd. But life does seem to be governed by surprisingly simple laws; and human beings, wherever and whatever they may be, do not greatly differ in essentials. That is the working hypothesis upon which art and religion, with imaginative genius to vitalize them, proceed. And let it be said of the theatre that a very short time in it will teach one how little fine clothes and fine manners may amount to. The theatre was for Shakespeare a laboratory where he worked—if but in a mimic sense—with human material. His method, his means to enlightenment, was to take a story and put the worth of it, its truth to nature, to the test of personal expression. The story might suffer; if it was not true to nature, it generally would. But Shakespeare was, on the whole, a most unconscientious story-teller, except when history bound him. Sometimes he would make a sacrifice to symmetry, as when, in *Measure for Measure*, he marries Isabella to the Duke; but he may have felt this to be poetic justice upon such a morally consistent lady. The story may be burked, neglected or finished off anyhow, as in *Much Ado About Nothing*, *Twelfth Night* and *As You Like It*. It may hang at the heels of the chief character, as in *Hamlet*. What men are, in fact, comes to concern him far more than what they do. Already in this pretty play of *Love's Labour's Lost* it instinctively concerns him, though not even doing but mere clever talk is his ostensible concern. And when he passes to the giant theme of *King Lear*, to the sweep of historic vision that is in *Antony and Cleopatra*, stretching his medium of expression till it seems to crack and break, he concerns himself, even then, with little which cannot be rendered into human passion, human pity—which cannot, in fact, be put to this laboratory test. He—literally—has no use for theories and abstract ideas. He is neither philosopher nor moralist, except as he must seem to be making his creatures one or the other. He is a playwright; he projects character in action, and with the truth of the one to the other his power and responsibility end. If this is the playwright's limitation, it is also his strength; for to this test of human response—not mimic, truly, but real; yet the mimic but reflects the real—all philosophy and morality must finally be put.

In this earliest essay, then, we may divine the dramatist to be; and we find dramatist putting wit and poet to the proof. Shakespeare will have set out to do his best by his creatures one and all; but while Berowne grows under his hand into a figure, finally, of some dramatic stature, while the Princess, simple, straightforward, shrewd, is made flesh and blood, in the speaking of seven lines, Navarre, though a natural focus of attention and discussing himself unsparingly, remains a bundle of phrases, and Dumain and Longaville have about the substance of echoes. Of the humbler folk; Costard for three-quarters of the play is the stage Fool, but suddenly, when he comes to the acting of his Worthy, we have:

COSTARD. I Pompey am, Pompey surnam'd the Big—
DUMAIN. The Great.

COSTARD. It is 'Great', sir; Pompey surnam'd the Great;
  That oft in field, with targe and shield, did make my foe
    to sweat;
  And travelling along this coast, I here am come by chance,
  And lay my arms before the legs of this sweet lass of France.
  If your ladyship would say, 'Thanks, Pompey', I had done.
PRINCESS. Great thanks, great Pompey.
COSTARD. 'Tis not so much worth; but I hope I was perfect:
  I made a little fault in 'Great'.

And these two last lines have, mysteriously and unexpectedly, given us the man beneath the jester. Then, with another thirty words or so, Costard (and Costard's creator) settles Sir Nathaniel the Curate, till now little but a figure of fun, snugly in our affections.

> There, an't shall please you; a foolish mild man; an honest man, look you, and soon dashed! He is a marvellous good neighbour, in sooth; and a very good bowler: but, for Alisander,—alas, you see how 'tis;—a little o'erparted.

And settles himself there yet more snugly in the doing it! Throughout the play, but especially towards the end, we find such outcroppings of pure dramatic gold.

Drama, as Shakespeare will come to write it, is, first and last, the projection of character in action; and devices for doing this, simple and complex, must make up three-quarters of its artistry. We can watch his early discovery that dialogue is waste matter unless it works to this end; that wit, epigram, sentiment are like paper and sticks in a fireplace, the flaring and crackling counting for nothing if the fire itself won't light, if these creatures in whose mouths the wit is sounded won't 'come alive'. To the last he kept his youthful delight in a pun; and he would write an occasional passage of word-music with a minimum of meaning to it (but of maximum emotional value, it will be found, to the character that has to speak it). His development of verse to dramatic use is a study in itself. He never ceased to develop it, but for a while the dramatist had a hard time with the lyric poet. The early plays abound, besides, in elaborate embroidery of language done for its own sake. This was a fashionable literary exercise and Shakespeare was an adept at it. To many young poets of the time their language was a new-found wonder; its very handling gave them pleasure. The amazing things it could be made to do! He had to discover that they were not much to his purpose; but it is not easy to stop doing what you do so well. Yet even in this play we may note the difference between the Berowne of

> Light seeking light doth light of light beguile;
> So ere you find where light in darkness lies
> Your light grows dark by losing of your eyes!

and of the soliloquy beginning

> And I forsooth in love ... [1]

Turn also from one of the many sets of wit to Katharine's haunting answer when Rosaline twits her with rebellion against Cupid:

ROSALINE. You'll ne'er be friends with him: he kill'd your sister.

KATHARINE. He made her melancholy, sad, and heavy;
And so she died: had she been light, like you,
Of such a merry, nimble, stirring spirit,
She might have been a grandam ere she died;
And so may you, for a light heart lives long.

Compare it with the set of wit that follows:

ROSALINE. What's your dark meaning, mouse, of this light word?

KATHARINE. A light condition in a beauty dark.
ROSALINE. We need more light to find your meaning out.
KATHARINE. You'll mar the light, by taking it in snuff;
 Therefore I'll darkly end the argument.

But Rosaline won't let her, and they manage to get
five more rather spicier exchanges. It is all very charming; the mere sound is charming, and a 'set of wit'
describes it well. Get a knowledge of the game and it
may be as attractive to watch for a little as are a few
sets of tennis. But pages on pages of such smart repartee
will not tell us as much of the speakers as those few
simple lines of Katharine's tell us—of herself and her
love of her sister, and of Rosaline too.

The play sets out, as we said, to be a flattering satire
upon such humours, and the playwright must set up
before he pulls down, break before he satirizes; and the
two processes do, doubtless, get mixed. Can we detect
a Shakespeare impatient, for a moment, with his pleasant
task? He has punned and joked his best.

BEROWNE. White-handed mistress, one sweet word with
 thee.
PRINCESS. Honey, and milk and sugar; there is three.
BEROWNE. Nay then, two treys, an if you grow so nice,
 Metheglin, wort and malmsey:—well run, dice!

Nor will he neglect the ever-satisfying humours of
cuckoldry.

KATHARINE. Veal, quoth the Dutchman:—is not veal a calf?
LONGAVILLE. A calf, fair lady?
KATHARINE.   No, a fair lord calf.
LONGAVILLE. Let's part the word.
KATHARINE.   No, I'll not be your half;
 Take all and wean it; it may prove an ox.

LONGAVILLE. Look, how you butt yourself in these sharp mocks!

Will you give horns, chaste lady? do not so.

KATHARINE. Then die a calf, before your horns do grow.

It amused him, no doubt, as it amused his audience; it is just too well done to have been done mechanically. But when, of a sudden, the Princess breaks out with

Are these the breed of wits so wondered at?

may we not hear for the moment his voice sounding through hers? For it is a barren business finally, and his fecund spirit could not long be subdued to it. With but little violence we could twist the play into a parable of his own dramatic progress. Even as Berowne at its end forswears

Taffeta phrases, silken terms precise,
Three-piled hyperboles, spruce affectation,
Figures pedantical . . .

so might Shakespeare be swearing to pass from them himself on towards the prose of *As You Like It* and the strong verse of *Julius Cæsar*. A notion not to be taken too seriously, perhaps. But a few years hence he is to let Hamlet record a taste for plays set down with as much modesty as cunning, with

no sallets in the lines to make the matter savoury, nor no matter in the phrase that might indict the author of affectation; but . . . an honest method, as wholesome as sweet and by very much more handsome than fine.

And certainly there are signs that, whether he knew it or not, the leaven was already working beneath this bright wit, this delight in words and their rhythm and melody, that was soon to turn a pretty speechifying Mercutio into the stark man of

> A plague of both your houses!
> They have made worms' meat of me: I have it,
> And soundly too. . . .

and the word-spinning Romeo into that doomed figure of

> It is even so? Then I defy you, stars!

The dramatist was in the making who was to fashion a Falstaff out of the old pickpurse of Gadshill, who was to pitch on the preposterous tale of *The Merchant of Venice*, and charge it (triumphantly, yet all but disastrously) with the passion of Shylock.[2]

But the producer must consider carefully just what the carrying-power of this embryonic drama is, and how he can effectively interpret to a modern audience the larger rest of the play. What life can his actors give to this fribble of talk and nice fantasy of behaviour? As satire it means nothing to us now. Where, then, are the prototypes of these cavaliers and ladies—of Armado and Holofernes, Moth and Nathaniel the Curate? We can at best cultivate an historical sense of them. There remains the verse, and the pretty moving picture of the action. Our spontaneous enjoyment will hang upon pleasant sounds and sights alone, sense and purpose apart. Really, it almost amounts to this! Better face the difficulty at its worst. Is there any surmounting it?

The Method of the Acting

IF only the last act were in question we should not need, I think, to qualify our Yes; for this is throughout as much Masque as play, it is meant to charm us as much by sight and sound as by story and character. To take one passage:

ROSALINE. What would these strangers? Know their minds,
  Boyet.
  If they do speak our language, 'tis our will
  That some plain man recount their purposes:
  Know what they would.
BOYET.   What would you with the princess?
BIRON.   Nothing but peace and gentle visitation.
ROSALINE. What would they, say they?
BOYET.   Nothing but peace and gentle visitation.
ROSALINE. Why, that they have, and bid them so be gone.
BOYET.   She says, you have it, and you may be gone.
KING.   Say to her we have measured many miles
  To tread a measure with you on the grass.
BOYET.   They say that they have measured many a mile
  To tread a measure with you on this grass.
ROSALINE. It is not so. Ask them how many inches
  Is in one mile: if they have measured many,
  The measure then of one is easily told.
BOYET.   If to come hither you have measured miles,
  And many miles, the princess bids you tell
  How many inches do fill up one mile.
BEROWNE. Tell her we measure them by weary steps.
BOYET.   She hears herself.

The action is implicit. Boyet must move, to the rhythm
of the verse, between one group and the other. He bids
fair to tread out a mile himself if the game last much
longer. But the two groups draw together after this, and
then break into couples. In a moment the music starts.
Instead of dancing, however, we have a dance of dialogue. The couples circle the stage to the sound of the
music, speaking their lines as they pass through the arc
the audience commands. Finally, Boyet, who can have
held his place in the centre, steps forward as chorus;
and for comment, full to the audience:

The tongues of mocking wenches are as keen
As is the razor's edge invisible,
Cutting a smaller hair than may be seen;
Above the sense of sense; so sensible
Seemeth their conference; their conceits have wings
Fleeter than arrows, wind, thought, swifter things.

The music stops. Four lines more, and the scene is over.

Now this has no dramatic value, properly so-called. It hardly furthers such plot as the play has; unless to make a tangle to be disentangled a scene later without more consequence can be called the furthering of a plot. It does not develop character. The dialogue is mere mischief. There is, of course, the satire; its edge is blunted by time. But if the music is clear and fine, as Elizabethan music was, if the costumes strike their note of fantastic beauty, if, above all, the speech and movements of the actors are fine and rhythmical too, then this quaint medley of Masque and play can still be made delightful. But it asks for style in the acting. The whole play, first and last, demands style. A vexingly indefinable thing, a hackneyed abracadabra of a word! One should apologize for bringing it into such a practical discussion as this pretends to be. Nor will the play as a whole, perhaps, be so entirely susceptible to its magic. But the theatre must deal in magic sometimes.

The conjecture that *Love's Labour's Lost* was first written for the delectation of a coterie of magnificent young men has been capped by the conjecture that some of them may have acted in it at the time. As custodians of the culture of the age, sponsors to this reborn mirroring art of the drama, they might well have recognized that they, in their own persons, apparel and conversation, mirrored and witnessed to that culture supremely. And they might, just for once, have condescended! They would have been

cast, of course, for Navarre, Berowne, Dumain and
Longaville. Some senior-junior might have been found
to fit Boyet, and someone who would modestly prefer
himself to Monsieur Marcade. Whether there is much
historical likelihood in the suggestion I do not know. If
so, the other parts would be played, we may suppose,
by professionals. There are the Masque and the antic
(the anti-Masque) in the last act; and we know that in
the great Court shows the lords and ladies did the
graceful dancing and left the grotesque to trained tum-
blers and dancers. One would like to complete the
picture by imagining the Princess and her ladies played
by some of those Maids of Honour, who used on occasion to 'friske and hey about'. Would not that Mistress
Fitton who—most historically—tucked up her skirts and,
cloaked like a man, marched out of Whitehall to meet
her lover, have been ready for once to play the boy and
act the woman? It could further be argued that the
dialogue for Navarre and his lords is of just such stuff
as those young bloods of culture delighted to try their
wits and tongues at; and that there is not much more
in it, nothing emotional (except for Berowne; and his
most emotional outburst is counted a later addition,
when the play was perhaps being revised for the public
stage), no impersonation, nothing that demands the professional actor with his greater comic or rhetorical force.
Navarre and his lords are, in modern stage slang, 'walking gentlemen'; but they need to walk magnificently and
to talk with a fine assurance. The historical question is
not pertinent to our present discussion, but these impli-
cations of it are. Whoever acted the play, it must have
been in these respects exquisitely done, or it could not
have endured its two hours' traffic, though its every joke
made a topical hit. Happy-go-lucky, with the hope of a
few guffaws for punctuation, could never have been a

method for this sort of thing. The audience, too, must have been attuned to its fantasies, to its exquisite passions. How passionate the Elizabethans were! They were capable—those that were articulate and responsive at all—of intellectual passion, as Englishmen have hardly been since. And when poetry and rhetoric display it in the charged atmosphere of the theatre, the effect—even the distant echo of it—is intense. Navarre and his

> little academe,
> Still and contemplative in living art .

are oath-bound fanatics; Berowne's gibing is but at the futility and hypocrisy of their professions.

> Warble, child: make passionate my sense of hearing .

says Armado, who is their caricature. Holofernes, that passionate latinist, Sir Nathaniel ridiculously emulating him, little Moth, with his piping and strutting, an incarnate mockery of them all, Costard reflecting their features in grimaces, their fine phrases in nonsense, the most reverberate things sounding hollow under the thwack of his bauble—all these, then, in accent and motion must be keyed to a sort of ecstasy, to a strange surpassing of this modern workaday world, if the play is to be anything at all but a sonata thumped out on a dumb piano, a picture painted by the colour-blind. A hard task for the actor; doubly hard, in that he must key up his audience too. For by time and subject it is all three hundred years' strange to us. We need an interpretation of absolute value; and that comes near to being a contradiction in terms. We must have a beauty of speech that will leave us a little indifferent to the sense of the thing spoken. Navarre and his friends and their ladies must show such distinction and grace that we ask no more pleasure in their company than that. Armado and the rest must command us by the very skill with which they remake mankind. It must indeed all be (to quote Berowne), if it is to exist at all,

as the style shall give us cause to climb in the merriness.

The Staging, Costume and Casting

THE play will profit little by any departure from Shakespeare's own staging; nor is this, in its simplicity, hard to deduce. A designer may shift the period of costume fifty years or so back—or forward, for that matter—if his taste dictate, and no great harm done. A certain grace may be added to Navarre and his friends by dressing them French fashion, or Italian. The Englishman was not famous for his taste in dress; though, if Portia may be trusted, he only made matters worse when he picked up notions abroad, his doublet in Italy, his round hose in France, his bonnet in Germany and his behaviour everywhere. But these scrupulous young men would be purists in tailoring too. And a comedy of affectations, of nice phrases, asks that its characters should be expressive to their boot-toes, significant in the very curl of a feather. None of the others are hard to picture. Shakespeare sets Armado before us clearly, the refined traveller from tawny Spain, dignified and mock-melancholy, carrying his rapier as might a conqueror of kingdoms, though for 'remuneration' to his messengers he cannot exceed three farthings, and must go shirtless, woolward for penance; he is black-suited, of course. Figure of fun as he is, though, his pride is not pinchbeck, nor must he look merely ridiculous. He sponges on no one, and hides his poverty all he can. When Costard infamonizes him among potentates—and the potentates, we may be sure, die with laughing—Shakespeare gives him great dignity in humiliation. We can picture Moth, that well-educated infant. Navarre, we may suppose, has made him page to the tall angular Spaniard for the fun of the contrast in the looks of them. Moth knows this well enough, be sure; and just how to make the best of his own share in the composition. He should not dress like Armado, that would coarsen the joke. He might still be wearing the King's livery. So might Costard, who makes a third in this conjunction, and has a flavour of Sancho Panza about him, even as Armado every now and then sets one thinking of that greater Don, yet in the womb of imagination. To complete this group we have the harsh, drab aspect of Holofernes; Sir Nathaniel, sober-suited but well-liking; and Dull, who is dull of countenance and clothing too. These will stand in sombre contrast to the choice-garmented Court and the rainbow beauty of the Princess and her ladies; till, for their show of the Nine Worthies, they too burst into flower, and into most wondrous and gaudy flowering.

The pictorial values in the pageantry of this last scene have their dramatic value too. The Russian maskings have been laid aside, cumbrously fantastic things, convenient cloakings. Yesterday Navarre and his friends were recluse philosophers; splendid even so, no doubt, but with a pallid splendour. Today they are in love and glowingly apparelled, in which symbolism their ladies can match them; and against this delicately blended colouring the village pageant tells crude and loud. Into the midst there suddenly steps Marcade, in black from head to foot. He hardly needs to speak.

> The king your father—
Dead, for my life!
> Even so, my tale is told.

Berowne takes order.

> Worthies, away! The scene begins to cloud.

And it must seem to cloud; the gay colours fading out, the finery folding about its wearers like wings. But this is not the end, for the end must not be melancholy. The countryfolk have yet to sing and dance their antic; a little crowd of them, dressed to match the

> daisies pied and violets blue,
> And lady-smocks all silver white,
> And cuckoo-buds of yellow hue . . .

The comedy of affectations comes to its full close upon notes of pastoral freshness and simplicity.

As with costume, so with scene; we shall gain nothing, we shall indeed be the worse for surrendering the freedoms of Shakespeare's stage. If we insist on placing and picturing the play's action now definitely here, now exactly there, we shall only be making complex what he has left simple, and find ourselves set to answer riddles which he never asked. The convention of place involved is 'about Navarre's Court'; outdoors, it seems to be, nothing more definite. The recluse King and his courtiers may walk there, the Princess may be met there, and no vows be broken; a pricket may be driven near for shooting, a pageant be shown there, a measure trod on the grass. Armado and his page walk there; so do the parson and the schoolmaster, unquestioned. Closer definition than this will be troublesome. The place, in fact, is not a place at all, within the modern scenic meaning. If we needs must paint the picture, it will need to be generalized, atmospheric, symbolic; the problem for a designer is quite a pretty one. Shakespeare, we may notice, hardly makes full practical demand upon the resources of the public theatre of the time. No use is made of the inner stage, though this might have served well for the Princess' pavilion. But the line:

> Whip to our tents as roes run o'er the land . . .

suggests a further flight. Except for one episode the play asks no more than a bare stage with a couple of openings to it, just such a provision as would be found in that great hall where we may suspect it was first acted. The scene of the philosophers' mutual discovery that they are, all four of them, forsworn and in love calls, however, for three hiding-places, of which one must be aloft; for Berowne says:

> Like a demi-god here sit I in the sky. . . .

But no harder mechanical problem faces the producer.[3]

This convention of place, and a similar freedom with time, encourages a very different method of construction from that proper to the theatre we know today, in which place, and even time, are positive and definite things. The dramatist, so set free, thinks more of his characters and less of their surroundings; he can manoeuvre them, absolved from such conformity, in the varied world of their own humours and passions. Elizabethan dramatic form has greater flexibility than ours; this, with its vehicle of verse (a further, more potent enfranchisement), gives it an emotional range which the modern dramatist must seek to compass by quite other means, by thrift of expression and tension sustained, by many hard economies. The scenic articulation of Shakespeare's later plays is masterly. They may seem loose-jointed, they are really supple and strong, delicate occasionally, never to be hacked at with impunity. *Love's Labour's Lost* is put together very simply; a little clumsily here and there, but alongside simplicity a little clumsiness will pass muster.

The main device—an obvious escape from monotony—is the alternating of one group of characters with the other, and of verse scenes with prose. The blending of the two groups at the last is as obvious a conclusion. But in the contriving of the changes we find him feeling his way—now missing it, now forcing it, truly—to incidental dramatic advantage. Elasticity of form was always to suit him best; it gave full play to his power of developing character.

We come quickly to a petty crudity of construction, of which a later Shakespeare might not have been guilty; it is amusing to note how conventional editing, covering the fault, makes it worse. Berowne, at the King's behest, departs, with Costard in charge, to seek Armado. But close upon his heels Armado appears. The editors mark a change of scene. Some shift the locality; some are for *Scene ii, the same.* The shift of locality supposes, of course, a regard for its realities which Shakespeare never had; but *Scene ii, the same* suggests an interval of time which is the last thing a swift-moving comedy requires at its outset. Let us see how Shakespeare himself gets over the difficulty he creates. He wants to divide two scenes of comedy by a scene of caricature. He does not think of localities. Berowne and Costard are to leave the stage in search of Armado. Armado is to appear a second later upon that same stage. This is clumsy, it will seem resourceless; it will affect his audience as a false note in music would, or a trip in a dance. Therefore he has Berowne leave the stage first, lets Costard lag behind for a little solitary funniment, and then bolt after Berowne. If the funniment raises a laugh, that breaks contact, as it were, and continuity. The bolting breaks the rhythm of movement: it also brisks up the end of the scene[4] and provides a contrast to the slow, stately entrance of Armado. All of which, together with the curiosity the

newcomer to the play arouses, will make us forget the
incongruity and will compensate for the clumsiness.
Shakespeare, of course, did not need to reason this out.
His dramatic instinct served him; so would anyone's. Act
the little passage as it is set down and its effect will be
automatic. A pity to comment upon it! But these in-
nocencies of drama must be protected against reasoning
men; the more innocent they are the more protection
they seem to need.

The rest of the play's comings and goings, by which
its action is spaced and divided, look likely enough, if
we do not insist upon looking at them through distorting
spectacles. They have not much other dramatic value.
If we want to make main divisions the play can be made
to fall well enough into three parts. The Quarto (as
usual) runs it through at a stretch; the Folio (as usual)
divides it into five acts. If four pauses are to mean four
intervals of distraction, this is a large allowance for so
slight a play. I should myself prefer the two, which would
leave Acts I and II of the Folio as a unit of exposition;
Acts III and IV for the uninterrupted working-out of the
simple plot; and Act V (which is longer than either of
the other two put together) for pageantry. This arrangement happens to exhibit some consistency in time. The
first part will mark the occasion—to all intent the day—
of the Princess' arrival; the second fills the following
morning; the third—Holofernes and Sir Nathaniel having dined presumably at midday—the afternoon following this.[5] But a producer might do well to abide by the
Quarto. It would at least compel him to keep the acting
brisk. The whole play could be put through in less than
two hours.

The Folio's Act IV does show, perhaps, a more complex significance of structure; there is what looks like a
deliberate use of the hunting subject as a link between

scene and scene. It is as if Shakespeare wanted to lead on—despite the variety and incongruity of the action here—without a marked break to the dominatingly important scene of the sonnet-reading and the four woodcocks in a dish. No disturbing climax, at any rate, intervenes between Berowne's soliloquy (which closes the third act) and this scene, which is the crisis properly evolved from it and the crisis of the play besides. How far this is deliberate, how far instinctive, may be profitless speculation; the producer should undoubtedly observe the effect.[6]

But the best of the play's craft is lodged in the dialogue; in its twists and turns, in the shifts of time and key, which are stage directions of the clearest sort. We have the brisking of a scene's end by such a piece of cross-fire as

BOYET.	Do you hear, my mad wenches?
MARGARET.	No.
BOYET.	What then, do you see?
ROSALINE.	Ay, our way to be gone.
BOYET.	You are too hard for me.

The author of *Twelfth Night* might have thought this a little crude; but it serves its purpose.

We find another hint to the actors to 'work up an exit', as the cant phrase has it, at the end of the scene of preparation for the pageant of the Nine Worthies. Dull, having spoken not a word nor understood one either, yet offers to make one in a dance and to play the tabor. Holofernes—no dancer, we presume!—turns down the offer with contempt. He departs. Armado has taken precedence of him and bidden him follow, so he departs pretty testily. But if Dull, left last, does not show us in a dozen steps what a chance they are missing— Shakespeare did not know the comedian's craft! And Shakespeare, both to his joy and sorrow, did!

Half the dramatic meaning of a passage may lie in the action it suggests.

ARMADO. Is not lead a metal heavy, dull and slow?

MOTH.   Minime, honest master, or rather, master, no.

ARMADO. I say lead is slow.

MOTH.   You are too swift to say so:
  Is that lead slow which is fired from a gun?

ARMADO. Sweet smoke of rhetoric!
  He reputes me a cannon; and the bullet, that's he;
  I shoot thee at the swain.

MOTH.   Thump, then, and I flee.

We must picture the long black barrel of a man, slow-gaited even in talk, and the little page, daintily at fence with him, and then off the stage at a bound. The art of it is akin to the artifice of a ballet.

The actor, in fine, must think of the dialogue in terms of music; of the tune and rhythm of it as at one with the sense—sometimes outbidding the sense—in telling him what to do and how to do it, in telling him, indeed, what to *be*. By the sense and sound together of the very first words spoken, Shakespeare is apt to make a character clear to actor and audience both.

  Boy, what sign is it when a man of great spirit grows melancholy?

Who, after the ample measure and high tone of that, could mistake Armado? See, again, his taciturn, self-conscious, amorous condescension and the wench Jaquenetta's mumchance allurement—the comic likeness and contrast of the two—hit out for us in a duet just forty-five words long.

    Maid.
    Man.

> I will visit thee at the lodge.
> That's hereby.
> I know where it is situate.
> Lord, how wise you are!
> I will tell thee wonders.
> With that face?
> I love thee.
> So I heard you say.
> And so, farewell.
> Fair weather after you.

—though, alas, Jaquenetta's country phrases have lost half their flavour for us now.

Shakespeare seems in the main content with the obvious contrast which the two groups and the shifts from verse to prose and back to verse again afford him. Prose is first brought into the play naturally enough by Costard and Dull and the reading of Armado's letter. The constricted pedantry of Armado's soliloquy ending the first act is followed pat—if no interval is allowed—by the strongest, simplest blank verse we have had yet. This effect is definitely dramatic, as of a sudden breeze of common sense blowing in. Berowne, it is true, has been preaching to us from this pulpit, but all tangled up himself in pun and antithesis. Even with the Princess and the ladies, however, we are back thirty lines later at

> The only soil of his fair virtue's gloss,
> If virtue's gloss will stain with any soil,
> Is a sharp wit match'd with too blunt a will....

at

> The young Dumain, a well-accomplish'd youth,
> Of all that virtue love for virtue lov'd...

and the like. Shakespeare's dramatic instinct has prompted the change; his art does not sustain it. He is still too occupied with the actual writing of the play, with himself, in fact, and his own achievements, to spare to his characters that superabundant strength which can let them seem to develop a life of their own. He relapses, therefore, to the thing he has learned how to do; as a man may find every new tune he whistles turning, despite him, into that one old tune he knows. He is still a little tangled—to make the point again—as his own Berowne is, in the affectations he is out to satirize.

But Berowne is the play's truly dynamic figure, and he and Shakespeare struggle out of the toils together. His

> And I forsooth in love . . .

lifts the play into living comedy. It is his comic ecstasy that gives life to the scene planned as the play's crisis, when all four men discover that they are all four in love. The rest of it is mere liveliness of wit and humour, and as arbitrary as a practical joke. The King, Longaville and Dumain are as much frigid phrase-makers in love as ever they were out of it. Shakespeare has still a last act to write, it may be argued. He must not anticipate the promise to woo

> In russet yeas and honest kersey noes . . .

But we shall not find him in the flush of his genius missing one chance because another must be waited for and hanging up a character's development. If characters are only to be moved by a series of jerks from one rigidity to the next, they will be more suitably played by marionettes than men. Man as marionette will be amusing for one scene, for a second less so; we shall find as much interest in a third look at him as in a look at any other stage furniture. And when we do reach the last act, Shakespeare, it seems, can make no more of his King, Longaville and Dumain in the end than he could at the beginning. There is no life in the fellows, and that's all about it. This lack of dramatic life, then, from which, let us own, the larger part of the play, and its more purposed part, suffers, its producer must face. It is, five-sixths of it, more decorative exercise than drama. It must therefore be given, as near as may be, what we have called an absolute value in sight and sound.

In yet one more respect the play may suffer by its transference from the Elizabethan stage. The acting of women by boys was in itself a contribution to these absolute values. Further, if we do not allow for the effect of this stringency upon Shakespeare's stagecraft even at its most mature, we shall be constantly at fault. Not that he seems to have felt it a drawback; among all his side-glances at actors and acting we find, I think, no hint that it irks him. It did not impoverish his imagination nor lead, on the whole, to any undue suppression of the womanly side in his plays.[7] It may influence his choice of subject; he does not trouble with domestic drama. Without doubt it determines what he will and will not ask woman characters and boy actors to do. Their love scenes are never embarrassing. They do not nurse babies. They seldom weep. He puts them, in fact, whenever he can, upon terms of equality with men; and women have been critically quick ever since to appreciate the compliment, not well aware, perhaps, how it comes to be paid them. For those conflicts of character which are the very life of drama he appoints weapons that each sex can wield with equal address; insight and humour, a quick wit and a shrewd tongue—the woman's the shrewder, indeed; in compensation, is it, for the softer advantages, the appealing charm, that his celibate theatre denied them? Out of a loss he plucks a gain.

Release from such reality drew him to set the relation of his men and women upon the plane of the imagination. It asked from the boy actors a skill, and a quite impersonal beauty of speech and conduct; those absolute qualities, in fact, of which we speak. The Elizabethan theatre lacked many refinements, but at least its work was not clogged nor its artistry obscured by the crude appeal of sex, from which the theatre today is perhaps not wholly free. No one wants to banish women from the stage; and it might not be an easy thing to do. But actresses may well be asked to remember what their predecessors achieved, and by what means.

In *Love's Labour's Lost*, however, the Princess and the ladies are not, and cannot be made, much more than mouthpieces for wit and good sense. As to love-making, the Princess gives us the cue with

> We have received your letters, full of love;
> Your favours, the ambassadors of love;
> And, in our maiden council, rated them
> At courtship, pleasant jest, and courtesy,
> As bombast, and as lining to the time:
> But more devout than this, in our respects,
> Have we not been; and therefore met your loves
> In their own fashion, like a merriment.

It is all to be gallant, open and aboveboard.

> Saint Cupid, then! and, soldiers, to the field.

They are to be leagued encounters; and no two of the lovers are ever alone. But how few of Shakespeare's love scenes now or later need it embarrass anyone to overhear! In more than one sense he habitually wrote for daylight effect upon an open stage. Passion and tragedy and high romance he has still to deal with; he has still to find out how to write Juliet and Isabella, Desdemona,

Cleopatra. But already the problem of Portia and Beatrice is solved, and Rosalind can be heard telling Orlando:

> You shall never take her without her answer unless you take her without her tongue.

The Text, and the Question of Cutting It

THE text presents practical difficulties, and one is fortunate to have Dr Dover Wilson's fresh work upon it in the new *Cambridge Shakespeare*. A flaw or so in method or result there may be; to set about correcting them with his own tools one would need uncommon skill. But it will be worth while to test his conclusions by their effect—as far as we can divine it—upon the play's staging, for good or ill. This is, in fact, the ultimate test to which many of these bibliographical subtleties must submit.

The pronouncement upon two imperfectly cancelled passages in Act IV, Scene iii, and Act V, Scene ii, answers to this test well. Some repetition in the first passage is patent; and, given a blue pencil and told to consider the dramatic upbuilding of the speech, who could make any other cut than that between lines 292 and 315? The textual muddle in the second is as obvious; and if Dr Dover Wilson's solution of it (though here, certainly, he but follows other editors) needs a stage-manager's support, it can be had for the sake of Berowne's

> Studies my lady? mistress, look on me.

For the dramatic intention is unmistakable. The King and Princess have made their exchanges, important and effective ones. If Berowne's and Rosaline's follow close, the importance of theirs must be lessened, unless some violent contrast is achieved, boisterous and quite out of key. But by the simple device of keeping these two chief characters still and silent while Dumain and Katharine, Margaret and Longaville, say their say—it must not be too long a say, nor important enough to demand our entire attention—we are put on the alert, held in suspense, brought to be wondering whatever will occur when the silence between them is broken. And an actual silence, a pause—no actor could help making one—must occur before

> Studies my lady? . . .

Thereafter, without effort or undue emphasis, or any illiberal self-assertion, Rosaline and Berowne, as they are meant to, top the scene.

This passage surely shows redrafting, and evidence of Shakespeare's more practised hand. But do the alterations run quite on Dr Dover Wilson's lines? Would Dumain begin, '*But* what to me . . . ' unless a previous speech had begun, '*And* what to me, my love?' It is unlikely that Shakespeare would ever have let the love-affairs even of two less important couples lapse in silence. May not Berowne's

> A twelvemonth! Well, befall what will befall. . . .

originally have followed upon Margaret's

> The liker you; few taller are so young.

And why, here and elsewhere, does Dr Dover Wilson bring in evidence the possible size of Shakespeare's writing-paper and the number of lines he could write on it? It was a scarcer substance with him, no doubt, than it is with his commentators. To suppose, though, that having taken a piece on which to write a new passage he could not stop till he had filled it . . . ! But Dr Dover Wilson *cannot* suppose this.

Another point of consequence is the Rosaline-Katharine confusion in Act II, Scene i. The suggested elucidation is best studied in the new *Cambridge Shakespeare* itself. It is as good as a detective story. Really, Scotland Yard should turn sometimes to our scientific bibliographers! Is one graceless to make any question of a verdict reached by such ingenuity? By the practical, dramatic test it stands, in the main. It is only that these nice investigations have the defects of their qualities; they tend to prove too much.

The case for this transference of the masks and the mistaken identity motive from Act II, Scene i, to Act V is, of course, strong upon several grounds. But to conclude from this, as Dr Dover Wilson does, that Shakespeare, making the alteration, meant to leave the earlier scene practically naked of everything but a dialogue between the King and the Princess, and a little questioning of Boyet by the young men and a little chaff for the young ladies, is to brand him as a very slack craftsman indeed. First, it is well-nigh inconceivable that he can let this scene pass, Rosaline and Berowne both present, and deny them an encounter. (Besides, without the first of the two passages between them, or something in its place, how is the King to read his letter?) The dialogue was originally written for Rosaline to play masked, no doubt. Later, Shakespeare did not care to change it; there was no compelling reason he should. She could just as well hold up her travelling-mask at Berowne's approach to tantalize him and fog him in his patronizing recognition of her. We must remember the space convention of the Elizabethan stage; the distance across it was anything in reason. Cannot we see him stalking the lady? And a mask in those days was a woman's accustomed protection in more senses than one.

The scene's second encounter between the two, how-ever, is redundant in itself, and of no constructional use; it is, indeed, an impediment to the action. Berowne and his fellows would not hang long behind when the King had departed; the Elizabethans appreciated ceremony in the theatre and out of it. But the stage, with its doors at the back, allowed for a many-paced exit. The three courtiers could follow with due observance if the ques-tions to Boyet began promptly; hardly otherwise. The redundancy, a certain clumsiness of construction, and, not least, the extreme artificiality of this 'set of wit' suggest it as part of an earlier growth, which, for some reason, was not clearly cut away. In its continuance, too, the dialogue shows every sign of having been hacked about. For instance,

> Good sir, be not offended:
> She is an heir of Falconbridge.

is halt, if not maimed.

So much, then, for the test of stage effect. But (before we pass on) among Dr Dover Wilson's own tests, are speech-headings such a safe guide to revision as he makes out? These are not, for the dramatist, a part of his play. Shakespeare, let us say, has a character in his head called Ferdinand, King of Navarre. If he wrote the play containing it at a sitting he might—though it is by no means inevitable—begin with one speech-heading and go on using it till the end. But it is likely enough that having made it 'Ferd:' on Monday and spent Tues-day at work upon Armado, on Wednesday he may be putting 'King' and on Friday 'Nav:' and even by the Monday following be using 'King' 'Nav:' 'Ferd:', which-ever comes first from his pen. He does not give a thought—why should he?—to such an entirely irrelevant matter. It will be the same with stage directions. While he is waiting for a scene to take fire in his mind, he may write with careful elaboration: *Enter the Princess of France with three attending ladies and three lords*, even as a schoolboy hopefully heads his paper with a copperplate 'Composition'. But when he sits down to it all-fired, *Enter the ladies* is good enough. Then he can get to work.

No doubt there are clues to be picked from these confusions that will not prove loose-ended. But when the critical editor begins, 'A natural and reasonable way of explaining . . . ,' one's concurrence is apt to be checked, even unfairly, by the overriding thought that what is reasonable to a critic is not therefore natural to a playwright.

We now come to the question of the permissible cutting of the text for modern performance, and no play in the canon presents greater difficulties. The principle is plain. A producer must take his stand with the first Cambridge editors and Garrick (Garrick! he may well exclaim) and resolve to 'lose no drop of the immortal man'. Still, no one need let his principles befool him. We need hardly hold sacred all that the printer has left us. The redundant passages in Act IV, Scene iii, and Act V, Scene ii, may go; Shakespeare's final intention is plain as a pikestaff.[8] There are besides a few sentences that are hopelessly corrupt; these we need not make a fuss about. But there are far more than a few that are nowadays almost, if not quite, incomprehensible, that require, at any rate, a professor and a blackboard as first aid. And over these principle and common sense come to loggerheads. For common sense does seem to urge: the average man in an audience will either understand these things or he won't; if he won't, cut them. The problem, however, is not quite so simple as this. If there is life in a play we cannot cut even ounces of flesh from it with impunity. If it is an articulated whole we cannot remove a joint and a sinew or two and not risk laming it. Thirty lines may be thirty lines and no more; but they may be—and they should be—an organic part of a scene.

For instance: Moth and Costard enter to Armado.

MOTH.   A wonder, master; here's a Costard broken in a shin.

ARMADO.   Some enigma, some riddle: come,—thy *l'envoy*; begin.

COSTARD.   No egma, no riddle, no *l'envoy*; no salve in the mail, sir. O, sir, plantain, a plain plantain! no *l'envoy*, no *l'envoy*: no salve, sir, but a plantain!

ARMADO.   By virtue, thou enforcest laughter; thy silly thought, my spleen; the heaving of my lungs provokes me to ridiculous smiling: O, pardon me, my stars! Doth the inconsiderate take salve for *l'envoy*, and the word *l'envoy* for a salve?

MOTH.   Do the wise think them other? Is not *l'envoy* a salve?

ARMADO.   No, page: it is an epilogue or discourse, to make plain. Some obscure precedence that hath tofore been sain. I will example it:

The fox, the ape, and the humble-bee,

Were still at odds, being but three.

There's the moral: Now, the *l'envoy*.

MOTH.   I will add the *l'envoy*; say the moral again.

ARMADO. The fox, the ape, and the humble-bee,

Were still at odds, being but three.

MOTH.   Until the goose came out of door,

And stay'd the odds by adding four.

Now will I begin your moral, and do you follow with my *l'envoy*.

The fox, the ape, and the humble-bee,

Were still at odds, being but three:

ARMADO. Until the goose came out of door,

Staying the odds by adding four.

MOTH.   A good *l'envoy*, ending in the goose; would you desire more?

COSTARD. The boy hath sold him a bargain, a goose, that's flat:—

Sir, your pennyworth is good, an your goose be fat.

To sell a bargain well is as cunning as fast and loose:

Let me see a fat *l'envoy*; ay, that's a fat goose.

ARMADO. Come hither, come hither: How did this argument begin?

MOTH.   By saying that a costard was broken in a shin.

Then call'd you for the *l'envoy*.

COSTARD. True, and I for a plantain; thus came your argument in:

Then the boy's fat *l'envoy*, the goose that you bought.

And he ended the market.

ARMADO. But tell me; how was there a costard broken in a shin?

MOTH.   I will tell you sensibly.

COSTARD. Thou hast no feeling of it, Moth: I will speak that *l'envoy*:

I, Costard, running out, that was safely within,

Fell over the threshold, and broke my shin.

ARMADO. We will talk no more of this matter.

Which last line alone we might expect an audience to appreciate!

What is a producer to do? How much of the stuff can any modern audience be brought to understand—even to understand, enjoyment apart? A glossary in the programme could give us first aid towards Moth's not very brilliant joke about Costard and shin, remind us that talk of a plantain leaf made the Elizabethans merry, even as a cry for brown paper and vinegar could once raise a laugh in Victorian farce—and a glossary will be needed for this very soon. But what can be done to recover such foundered word-play as

No egma, no riddle, no *l'envoy*, no salve in the mail, sir.

or to give life and sense to Moth's

Is not *l'envoy* a salve?

When we come to

The fox, the ape, and the humble-bee . . .

we can, grown desperate, find Folio authority for a cut. The new *Cambridge* editors insist that it is an obviously topical joke, its application long lost; we might get rid of it upon that ground.[9]
But—worse and worse!—we next come to elaborate jesting about a goose and a market.

Should a producer expunge the whole thing and bring Costard on to hear at once of his enfranchisement? This may well be the lesser evil. But one cannot thus eviscerate a scene and expect to see no wound. Here is an effect gained by the resolving of the long Armado-Moth duet into a trio, by rounding off the sententious folly and nimble mockery with the crude humour of the clown. The dialogue passes from prose to rhymed couplets; then becomes gay with jingle, which Costard jollily burlesques in that long lolloping metre. We must think of it all in terms of music, of contrasts in tone and tune, rhythm and breaking of rhythm. There is the value of the picture too, set before us and held for its minute or two; of the egregious dignity of Armado, Moth delicately poised, and Costard square-toed and cunning, not such a fool as he looks. All this has histrionic value, the sheer sense of the dialogue apart. All plays exist, plots and character-schemes beside, as schemes of sound, as shifting pictures, in decoration of thought and phrase, and the less their dependence on plot or conflict of character the more must they depend upon such means to beauty and charm. These 'set pieces' may be loosely and easily contrived, so that they still give an illusion of life; and we must never be made overconscious of them, or the charm may vanish, even though the beauty remain. But in this play, as we have seen, much depends on them. We are, indeed, never very far from the formalities of song and dance. The long last act is half Masque and half play; and in song and dance the play ends.

Therefore, it being understood that pretty picture and pleasant sound alone will never suffice, before sentence is passed on a difficult passage it might well be put upon probation. Let the actors see what they can make of it by adroit movement and the nice turning of a phrase. There is danger here. Released from that troublesome obligation to make current sense of his goings-on, the actor too readily turns acrobat; and the audience, come to do their duty by Shakespeare, hardly expect to make much sense of the stuff anyhow. Better cut half the play than act any of it on these terms; but better, then, not act it at all. There are passages, however (though the one we have just quoted is not in its entirety one of them), which do yield something to such treatment. Who, with an ear for the music and rhythm of fine prose, will not take pleasure, for instance, in the very sound of

ARMADO. Go, tenderness of years! take this key, give enlargement to the swain, bring him festinately hither; I must employ him in a letter to my love.

MOTH. Will you win your love with a French brawl?

ARMADO. How meanest thou? brawling in French?

MOTH. No, my complete master; but to jig off a tune at

the tongue's end, canary to it with your feet, humour it with turning up your eyes; and sigh a note and sing a note as if you swallowed love with singing love, sometimes through the nose, as if you snuffed up love by smelling love; with your hat penthouse-like over the shop of your eyes; with your arms crossed on your thin belly-doublet like a rabbit on a spit: or your hands in your pockets, like a man after the old painting; and keep not too long in one tune, but a snip and away. These are complements, these are humours, these betray nice wenches that would be betrayed without these, and make them men of note—do you note me?—that are most affected to these.

ARMADO. How hast thou purchased this experience?

MOTH. By my penny of observation.

ARMADO. But O—but O,—

MOTH. The hobby-horse is forgot.

ARMADO. Call'st thou my love hobby-horse?

MOTH. No, master; the hobby-horse is but a colt—and your love perhaps a hackney. But have you forgot your love?

ARMADO. Almost I had.

MOTH. Negligent student! learn her by heart.

ARMADO. By heart, and in heart, boy.

MOTH. And out of heart, master: all those three I will prove.

ARMADO. What wilt thou prove?

MOTH. A man, if I live: and this—by, in, and without, upon the instant. By heart you love her, because your heart cannot come by her; in heart you love her, because your heart is in love with her; and out of heart you love her, being out of heart that you cannot enjoy her.

It is pure *bravura*; it hangs up the action, it hardly develops character; Shakespeare the full-fledged dramatist would not have written it. We may indeed compare it to an *aria* in an opera. It calls for a comparable execution, an audience should get the same sort of pleasure from it. And if the musical value is not quite as great—well, we mostly miss the words of the *aria* as a rule.

To make a tentative list of the passages with which nothing can be done, of the bits of dead wood, one may call them:

> ARMADO. I love not to be crossed.
> MOTH. He speaks the mere contrary, crosses love not him.

Moth's line at least might come out. The joke can't be conveyed, nor is it worth the conveying.

The dancing horse is dead past resurrection. If a ruthless pencil does away with the lines that lead up to the point and the two that drop away from it, can the most fervid Shakespearean—more royalist than his king—complain?

The reference to the ballad of the King and the Beggar might go too. On the other hand, anyone who would mangle the discourse upon the four complexions, if it were only that he might so deprive us of Armado's

> Define, define, well-educated infant.

is a butcher and botcher of texts.

The whole passage between Boyet, the ladies and Costard in Act IV, Scene i, which begins with the now cryptogrammatic pun,

> Who is the suitor? who is the suitor?

—if one pronounces it 'sewtor' the joke is lost, so it is to a modern audience if one calls it 'shooter'—asks at first sight for drastic treatment. Say we surmount this first obstacle, eke out the everlasting jokes about cuckoldry

that follow with a wink or two and a nod, we shall still
be utterly lost in the tangle of talk—yet more equivocal
in every sense—about archery and bowling. Nevertheless, if one is not to truncate the whole scene and end
it with the Princess' departure—and this is structural
alteration and inadmissible—it may be better to go
through with the gibberish, to let it seem so if it must.
For again, consider the action, the lively picture; Boyet
surrounded by the teasing girls, Costard ecstatic at the
encounter! And are we to miss the little singing dance
with which Rosaline takes leave? Apart from the charm
of it—the girl and the gay old courtier answering and
counter-stepping each other—and apart from the value
of this little turmoil of rhythmic gaiety before we drop
to our first experience of Holofernes and his pedantry,
Shakespeare is bringing Rosaline by degrees to her due
place of importance in the play, and no item of the
process should be omitted.

As to Holofernes and Sir Nathaniel, it is a good part
of the fun of them that neither the innocent Dull, nor
we, can make out half the time what they are talking
about. No need then, after all, to be troubled by

Priscian a little scratched . . .

or even by the mystery of the charge-house on the top
of the mountain. But what can—what ever *can*!—be
made of Moth's pleasantries about the five vowels
and the horn-book (yet once again a cuckold's horn-
book!) in the first scene of the last act? If ever a
passage could serve in a competition with a prize given
to the set of actors that extracted some legitimate effect
from it, this could! Nor is it of any constructive consequence, nor does it add one stroke of character.
Why not pass boldly then, from Costard's achievement
of

honorificabilitudinitatibus: thou are easier swallowed than a flap-dragon.

to

> Arts-man, preambulate . . .

and so to the play's business?

But really there is nothing more, save a line or two of obvious indecency easily left out, that the producer need wish to conjure away. There remains but to question one apparent corruption of text, which does obscure the action at an important point, then to point out one or two possible pitfalls in the casting of the parts, and this prefacing, grown longer than the play itself, may end.

The King, that noble gentleman and Armado's very good friend, having set on his butt to provide the entertainment of the Nine Worthies, encourages his guests in the doubtless far better entertainment of making outrageous fun of him. By the standards of the time this may not have seemed to be such very caddish behaviour. We recall the practical jokes played by the Duke and Duchess on Don Quixote. Cervantes could have commented, as Shakespeare cannot; but he let the business speak for itself. Still, it is possible that Shakespeare, though flattered, no doubt, by the approval of his own play's very select audience, had his private opinion upon this aspect of their gentility. Certainly, when the final trick is played on Armado, it is he, fantastic fool as he is, who shines out as the best gentleman amongst them, even as Don Quixote shone. The manner of the trick itself, however, is all confused in the text as we have it, and its matter is somewhat obscure. Berowne incites Costard to bring Armado's play-acting to utter grief by rushing on distraught with the sudden news that the wench Jaquenetta is cast away, is two months gone,

Armado the culprit. The stage directions that make this clear Dr Dover Wilson has most justly restored. And as justly he restores to Armado the line that he must speak to give point to the interruption:

> The party is gone.
> Fellow Hector, she *is* gone. . . .

exclaims Costard. But the effect is still incomplete. The first line must surely be a part of Hector the Worthy's speech (this Dr Dover Wilson does not hold). Where is the comic incongruity of Costard's twist of the phrase otherwise? It is such an obvious trick; neither Costard, nor Shakespeare at this moment, could neglect it. One suspects a pun in 'party'. It can mean an antagonist, Achilles against Hector. An intermediate line may be missing; it cannot be restored unless someone should discover a colourable original of the pageant. But at least the incident and its business can be rightly outlined in action.

Further, it is surely clear—though to many editors it does not seem to be—that in the accusation poor Armado *is* most scandalously 'infamonized'. Where would be the joke else? The King and Princess, the courtiers and ladies, must, most of them, know by this time of his ridiculous adoration of this country wench; and we have seen how she treats him. Armado a hypocrite! The whole character is destroyed at a blow. If there were a guilty party, we might rather suspect Costard, who did 'confess the wench'. But it may all be a joke. Armado, at least, is convinced so, for back he comes before the play's end, quite his magnificently absurd self again. And he, faithful among the faithless, will be a votary still; but to philosophy no longer, to the plough, to rusticity. We can imagine him, though hardly a great success in the furrows behind a team, sitting like Don Quixote beneath a tree—again the comparison is irresistible—and piping to the virginal Jaquenetta. Though, if Moth's estimate of the young lady's character should, after all, be the right one, Shakespeare is a finished ironist already.

As to the casting of the comic parts; only with Costard is it not plain sailing. Holofernes is pendant incarnate, and Sir Nathaniel simple parson. Jaquenetta is a country wench and Dull is the village constable. But Costard, swain though he is,[10] smacks both of Court-jester and stage clown. Shakespeare had often to make use of these chartered comedians. Sometimes, as in *Twelfth Night, As You Like It* and *King Lear*, he can fit them to the play. Sometimes, as there is evidence, they were a sore trial to its integrity. Costard is the conventional figure thinly disguised, and he may quite rightly be played so. In his very first scene, though he is Armado's man brought by the constable for correction, he takes all the jester's liberties with the King.

KING.   Peace!
COSTARD. Be to me and every man that dares not fight.
KING.   No words!
COSTARD. Of other men's secrets, I beseech you.

His attitude towards the Princess is the same. The actor, then, is given a character to assume for the play's consistency's sake; he must keep within it about as much as a low comedian did in Victorian farce or in Edwardian musical comedy. But no more. The play does not need another slow-spoken countryman. For that we have Dull, sparse of words, and heavy of gait. Costard's is a nimble wit; we must feel that for diversion he makes himself out to be more of a fool than he is. And the actor himself must be skilful of speech and light of touch, as good jesters and stage clowns were.

The Music

THE indications of music and of the one dance are plain enough. Moth's 'Concolinel' of Act III, Scene i, stands for a song, which no research has yet tracked. How anyone can doubt this it is hard to see. In the earlier scene Moth is asked to sing. There is no point whatever in his here disappointing Armado and the audience too with a comic catch-phrase. And why should Armado's comment upon it be

Sweet air!

Moreover, the stage direction in the Folio definitely says, *A song*. If what Shakespeare wrote or chose cannot be found, the producer must do the next best thing and make such a choice for himself as Shakespeare might have made. Many of the sources from which he picked ballads when he wanted them are open to us. A pity to have to do it, but obviously better than to leave a gap in the scene. The recurrent lightening of the play with lyrics sung or said is a part of its artistic economy.

The dance the blackamoors play, that Rosaline and the ladies will not respond to, may well be a 'French brawl'. A pity to miss the canarying with the feet; but the music probably lasts, as we have noted—the players in the background—till the finish of Boyet's apostrophe to the ladies' jigging tongues.

For the end we have song and dance both. *Enter all*, say Quarto and Folio too. The play finishes, as a play of merry-making should, with everyone ranged for our last look at them. The simplest sort of a thing will serve best. Pedantry, cleverness, set poses, nice speaking, are all dropped. Armado, the incorrigible, the votary still, will have it, of course, that we are to hear a dialogue by the two learned men. The two learned men are to be found but a moment later dancing a hay with the best. Moth may sing the Spring song and Jaquenetta Winter's. Dull, it turns out, can do marvels on the pipe and tabor. Costard too, no doubt.

In fact, as there is no curtain to descend, no other-world of illusion to hide, the actors are already putting off the characters so lightly worn, and telling us that, after all, it is only a play. No, Armado does not dance. It is as if, the revels over, he stalked forward to speak an epilogue:

> The words of Mercury are harsh after the songs of Apollo. . . .

and could get no further. Are they ready to mock him again? Then he bows to the quality:

> You, that way; we, this way.

shepherds his motley flock and stalks after them.

1926

Notes

1 Which, says Dr Dover Wilson, belongs to the play's revising. But this does not invalidate my point; rather the contrary.

2 He pitched, we may say, upon two preposterous tales, and redeemed the second by the romantic beauty of Portia.

3 And at this point in the play, also at this particular point in the scene, Dr Dover Wilson scents revision. It may well be that Berowne, like the King and Longaville, originally hid on the stage level. But the stagecraft as we have it is worth examination. When Berowne is aloft Dumain does not come into his view till some minutes after Longaville espies him. This suggests that, if and when the play was revised for a public theatre, the tree (of some editors) to be climbed was no more than the gallery at the back of the stage, though a

property tree might have been set against it, so that he would appear to be in its branches. Isolated property trees that can be climbed must be very solid affairs indeed. Berowne knows of Longaville's approach, for the King names him. But Longaville's only warning of Dumain's is 'Company! Stay!' Then he bolts to hiding, not having himself seen, perhaps, who the intruder is. This is likely, for Shakespeare was from the beginning too good a dramatist to duplicate an effect. It would seem as if the stage stayed apparently empty for a moment, while Berowne said:

> All hid, all hid; an old infant play.

Next that Dumain entered, walking slowly down to the accompaniment of

> Like a demi-god here sit I in the sky.
> And wretched fool's secrets heedfully o'er-eye.

At which point Berowne sees his back:

> More sacks to the mill!

Then identifies him:

> O heavens, I have my wish!
> Dumain transform'd: four woodcocks in a dish!

With all the emphasis on *four*, a climax well worked up!

4 One cannot be always defining the sense in which one is using this word; the context, one hopes, will make it plain. Here, of course, it implies a division of dialogue.

5 There are some signs of confusion in Act III, Scene i. Berowne (and possibly at the moment Shakespeare) seems to think the Princess is coming to hunt in the afternoon. As it happens, she comes in the morning, only a minute or two after Berowne himself has started for his ride.

6 Hence he should not tolerate an interval, even if he allow a pause, after the Folio's Act III.

The scene following the soliloquy, after recording Berowne's distracted spurring of his horse uphill (the audience can easily tell that it was he, if he has just been before them, booted and spurred, whip in hand), goes practically straight to the hunting subject. This is returned to for a finish by means of a shout within (which, I believe, should rather be 'shoot' within) and Costard's running out with a halloo. The next scene begins,

> Very reverend sport, truly . . .

and ends with

> Away! the gentles are at their game. . . .

while Berowne begins the scene following with

> The king he is hunting the deer. . . .

Conventionalized time is used, of course, throughout the four scenes. This, moreover, is all we hear of the day's hunting. But it is enough for Shakespeare. A hunt is toward; and no more excuse is needed in an English countryside or an English theatre—nor would be in the most categorical of plays—for anyone and everyone to turn up incontinently.

7 Except in the actual fewness of women's parts, for which the fewness of the boy apprentices allowed may be accountable.

8 It is the present redundancy, of course, that we keep.

9 But is this so? I can imagine an American editor three hundred years hence testing the verse which begins,

> I never saw a purple cow. . . .

for an allusion to President Wilson. Was not Roosevelt called a bull-moose? But the mere truth is that sixty million people or so once thought that funny in itself.

10 And this need imply nothing rustic about him. He is Armado's body-servant merely.

Notes

Notes

Notes

Notes

Notes

Notes

Notes

Notes

Notes